RELIGION AND PHILOSOPHY IN GERMANY

Heinrich Heine, German lyric poet and literary critic, was born in Düsseldorf in 1797. Originally of Jewish descent, in 1825 he renounced this faith to become a Christian. He lived alternately at Hamburg, Berlin, and Munich. From 1831 until his death in 1856 he lived for the most part in Paris, and it was during this period that he contributed generously to two Parisian journals, *Europe Littéraire* and the *Revue des Deux Mondes*. It was in the latter of these that the prose fragments contained in this volume were first published. GEDICHTE, the first collection of his poetry, was followed by BUCH DER LIEDER, NEUE GEDICHTE, and ROMANZERO. These contain some of the best-loved German lyrics. Heine produced a number of characteristic prose works including REISEBILDER (4 vols.), GESCHICHTE DER NEUREN SCHÖNEN LITERATUR IN DEUTSCHLAND (2 vols.), DER SALON (4 vols.), and VERMISCHTE SCHRIFTEN (3 vols.). His complete works were published posthumously at Hamburg (1861-1866) in twenty-one volumes, and a great number of these have been translated into English and adapted for the present-day reader.

Religion and Philosophy in Germany

A Fragment

By HEINRICH HEINE

Translated by
John Snodgrass

Foreword by
Dennis J. Schmidt

State University of New York Press

First Published in America in 1882 by
Houghton Mifflin and Company

Published by
State University of New York Press, Albany

© 1986 State University of New York

For information, address State University of New York
Press, State University Plaza, Albany, N.Y., 12246

Library of Congress Cataloging-in-Publication Data

Heine, Heinrich, 1797–1856.
    Religion and Philosophy in Germany.

    Translation of: Zur Geschichte der Religion und
Philosophie in Deutschland.
    Includes index.
    1. Philosophy, German.   2. Germany—Religion.
I. Title.
B2523.H413   1986   193   85-27675
ISBN 0-88706-282-2
ISBN 0-88706-283-0 (pbk.)

CONTENTS

FOREWORD BY Dennis J. Schmidt   vii

TRANSLATOR'S NOTE   xxiii

PREFACE TO FIRST FRENCH EDITION   1

PREFACE TO FIRST GERMAN EDITION   8

PREFACE TO SECOND GERMAN EDITION   9

PART FIRST: Germany Till Luther's Time   19

PART SECOND: From Luther to Kant   59

PART THIRD: From Kant to Hegel   105

APPENDIX   165

FOREWORD *by* DENNIS J. SCHMIDT

HISTORIES which regard their task as the simple and uncompli-cated narrative of a finished and by-gone past frequently find themselves quickly transformed into documents and relics of a new past, and of only an antiquarian interest. But a different sort of history, one that touches upon something vital in the life of history and the mind and so does not freeze itself in its own present, is continually able to speak beyond its own age and to awaken interest in its topic and message. Heine's study on the history of religion and philosophy in Germany certainly ranks among the best examples of just such a history which, in look-ing back, raises and addresses questions that reach far in advance of itself. Many histories of German thought have been written since Heine wrote this one for a French audience in 1834; most of those others now seem covered with dust while Heine's text reads as fresh as one composed today.

Part of the enduring appeal of this book is no doubt due to its jargon-free presentation of complex theological and philosophical positions. Heine's populist sensibilities and political mission bred in him the conviction that the true measure of an idea is first found in its legacy and impact upon the cultural life of a people. Fueled by this conviction he looks upon himself as the bearer of the German tradition whose role it is to translate and help interpret that tradition, thereby pro-moting and accelerating the very best of that tradition. To this end, he wrote with an eye to a readership beyond the walls of the ivory tower. The eloquent and often witty style of this text is certainly another factor contributing to its appeal and youth. Heine was a leading literary critic in his day and still remains among Germany's greatest poets, one whose verse has been turned to songs by Schubert, Schumann, and Wolff to name but a few inspired by the musicality of his language. But while some of the charm of this text comes from Heine's ability to reach his audience and his obvious delight and virtuosity with language, its special excellence is not that it is an uncommonly readable presentation of the German intellectual tradition from Luther to Hegel, but is found in the original contribution that it makes to the tradition of which it speaks.

There are three issues which dominate Heine's concerns and so determine the matrix of his critical history of German thought: the nature and place of the divine; the goal of a more harmonious life and the preparation for the social revolution which would make such a life possible; and the power and genius of language. In the end, none of these issues takes priority over the others, since in the history of a culture they are ineluctably entangled in a dialectic. One might even say that, for Heine, the motor of history, its active life and decisive turns, is found in the progressive unfolding of our understanding of these three ideas. That does not mean that Heine is willing to let the real and practical life of peoples evaporate and be replaced by intellectual history; it means rather that his intention is to affirm the reality of theory and ideas as underpinning the active life of people. The shape of things that are and are to come is most clearly outlined in the interactive history of these three themes. To win a positive place in such a history is to have made some significant contribution to one or more of these themes, and so to have propelled the dialectic of history forward on at least one of its axes.

The first, and greatest, such push in this history comes from Luther who emerges here as the deepest influence upon the German mind and character. It is Luther who sets Germany back on the track to what eventually becomes its "open secret" — pantheism — and this is an event of revolutionary significance that sets the tone for things to come. In the first book of this text Heine shows how Christianity, which in the Middle Ages spread like an "infectious disease" throughout the Roman empire, never succeeded in extinguishing the native pantheist religion of heathen Germany. This earlier pre-Christian religion saw the earth as a place of the gods: "Its mysteries and symbols were referable to a worship of nature; in every element men adored some marvellous being, every tree revealed a deity, all the phenomena of the universe were informed by divinity. Christianity reversed this view; nature, ceasing to bear the impress of the divine, became diabolised." Christianity, in the form of the Roman Church, turned these earthly pagan gods into devils and repudiated all that was of the earth, so that flesh and body, which were once celebrated, are now annihilated. Not the earth, but heaven, is the home of God who rules from above through his earthly representatives, the priests. Characterized by a deistic denial of the divinity of nature and the corresponding spiritualist negation of the body, Christianity is hostile to human nature on two scores: it provides the basis for political despotism insofar as it grants a special authority on what is right and just to a few who are said to be nearer the divine, and it represses the healthy expression of the body and the sensuous admiration of beauty. Priests are then a ready ally of political authority, while all people are alienated from their original nature.

Attacking the authority of the priests and the Church, and rehabilitating the body, Luther knocked down the two most significant obstacles to the free and harmonious life, thereby inaugurating a movement that will not come to a close for some three centuries. After this religious revolution German culture is ready for its next critical, in this case philosophical, moment. But from Luther forward, the essential direction of history is visible and Germany seems inexorably destined to yet another, this time political revolution, one that Heine describes at the close of the third book:

> German thunder is of true German character: it is not very nimble, but rumbles along somewhat slowly. But come it will, and when ye hear a crashing such as never before has been heard in the world's history, then know that at last the German thunderbolt has fallen. At this commotion the eagles will drop dead from the skies and the lions in the farthest wastes of Africa will bite their tails and creep into their royal lairs. There will be played in Germany a drama compared to which the French Revolution will seem but an innocent idyll. At present, it is true, everything is tolerably quiet; and though here and there some few men create a little stir, do not imagine these are to be the real actors in the piece. They are only little curs chasing one another round the empty arena, barking and snapping at one another, till the appointed hour when the troop of gladiators appear to fight for life and death.
>
> And the hour will come. As on the steps of an amphitheatre, the nations will group themselves around Germany to witness the terrible combat.

Despite the ominous sound of these words in light of events in Germany a century later, Heine's vision of the coming social change initiated by Luther, and furthered by Kant and Hegel, was not intended as the prophesy of a great evil to come; it was rather a declaration of the depths of the upheavals that were to follow in the social world from the revolution in thought outlined here. Heine has no doubt that these revolutions in thought will inevitably produce political actions for "thought precedes action, as lightning does the thunder." This book traces the history of the revolutions in thought which start with Luther; the last pages promise and warn of the thunder to come. Heine's feelings about the coming upheavals is never unambiguous. His vision of the future of humanity clearly owes much to Hegel's sense of progress and to Saint-Simon's evolutionary utopianism. From his discussion of Luther it is already evident that he sees the goal of history to be a paradise where body and spirit are reconciled, where the harmony among men so deeply wounded by the Christian world has been restored, and where nature is once again understood to be divine. But Heine is never intoxicated with the idea of revolution: the text ends with a sober reminder that the goddess of wisdom is the goddess dressed and armed for war. Long before Horkheimer and Adorno write the *Dialectic of Enlightenment* Heine is troubled by the risks and possible price of what he sees as promise and hope. He would doubtless agree with Hölderlin's remark that "where danger is, there rescue grows."

Regardless of the ultimate outcome of the German revolution Heine does argue that its roots must be traced back to Luther, who is "not only the greatest, but most German man of our history." But Luther's achievement is not exhausted by the overthrow of the yoke of authority found in deism and the overcoming of the unnatural antagonism that Christian spiritualism set between body and spirit. Rather his greatest achievement in Heine's eyes is one that at first sounds somewhat strange, namely that "he created the German language." Luther's trans-

lation of the Bible is the true act of his genius since to do so
required that the language, grammar, and syntax of German be
stretched and changed to accommodate what was previously
unexpressible in German. In this way Luther changed the possi-
bilities of what could be said and thought in German, and by
translating the one book available to every corner of Germany
he gave the German people a language that reached beyond the
division of regional dialects. Such an act is not merely an act of
literary and linguistic creativity, it is a powerful political act as
well, one which made a literary unity of a politically and religiously divided nation. Furthermore, since the Bible was one
book available to even the poorest classes "they have no need of
any special learned instruction to enable them to express themselves in a literary style. This circumstance will, when the
political revolution takes place in Germany, result in strange
phenomena. Liberty will everywhere be able to speak, and its
speech will be Biblical." Language is always among the deepest
and most active forces in praxis and the life of a culture. The
language of Germany, though later shaped by Lessing and
Goethe and Heine himself, remains profoundly Lutheran and
this is his true lasting achievement.

Like Hegel before him and Heidegger later, Heine regards
German as the philosophic language par excellence; it is particularly well suited to the tasks of both speculation and disclos-
ing the secrets of nature: "In no other language could nature
reveal its most secret work as well as in our beloved German
mother-tongue." Consequently, once Germany has inherited its
language from Luther, philosophy rather than religion eventually becomes the leading revolutionary force in the struggle of
liberation from deism and spiritualism. For a long time after
Luther both philosophy and religion, though each autonomous,
are found to express the same truth, but once the speculative

dimension of the German language takes hold and religion makes an appeal to philosophy in order to justify itself it loses its autonomy and begins its decline. The philosophic arena is then the next place where we witness the struggle over the key concerns of history.

Kant is the hero of this second revolution, and so it is not until we arrive at him that the philosophic revolution finally erupts. But Kant is not the first philosopher in whom we feel the first breezes of the future. It is rather Spinoza who makes the first real contribution to bringing nearer the goal of a more harmonious life. Quietly, without the fanfare accorded the mighty Kant as the greatest terrorist in the realm of the mind and as executor of the deist God, Spinoza enters this history's gallery of heroes. His merit is not to have denied God as his contemporaries accused him of doing, but to have divinized man. By demonstrating the oneness of all substance and claiming that this substance is divine, infinite, and absolute, Spinoza provides the most sublime and lasting outline of the intelligible structure of the pantheistic world. With Spinoza's great pantheistic synthesis of extension and thought, matter and spirit can once again be seen as the unity and whole that nature would have them be. In this way he provides a vision of, and positive argument on behalf of the ideal world to come. Here we see a way to heal the wounds caused by spiritualism's presumptuous reign over the body and deism's denial of all that is natural.

In a curious way, Spinoza comes too early, and history is not yet ready for him. Nevertheless, what he teaches is indispensable and will have to be said again in the light of events yet to come. Indeed Spinoza does resurface again and again modified and in the guise of later thinkers: Goethe is called the "Spinoza of poetry," and the fundamental principle of German Idealism and the philosophy of identity is said to be essentially no different than the doctrine of Spinoza. But Spinoza himself lacked something essential, something that only history could provide; namely, a dramatic break in tradition, a rupture in history itself that would prepare history for what he has to offer. Heine announces this coming break with the past at the close of the second book in a passage that smacks of Nietzsche writing fifty years later:

> . . . it is the old Jehovah himself that is preparing for death. We have known him so well from his cradle in Egypt . . . . We have seen him migrate to Rome, the capital, where he abjures all national prejudices and proclaims the celestial equality of all nations . . . and intrigues ceaselessly till he attains supreme authority, and from the Capitol, rules the city and the world, *urbem et orbem*. We have seen how growing more spiritualized, he becomes a loving father, a universal friend of man, a benefactor of the world, a philanthropist; but all this could avail him nothing!
>
> Hear ye not the bells resounding? Kneel down. They are bringing the sacraments to a dying God!

Not until Kant, who fashions the "sword that slew deism in Germany," is history ready for a vision of the future. However, from Kant forward, a new epoch in the history of thought begins.

To fully appreciate Heine's estimation of the depth and significance of the revolution represented by Kant one need remember a fundamental tenet of Heine's own philosophic position, namely, that thought and action cannot be separated, and that thought always precedes and determines the course of action. This idea is certainly not original to Heine, the priority of theory in the reciprocal relation of theory and praxis is a key element in the Hegelian system and becomes a central issue in Marx's critique of Hegel, but nowhere is theory so quickly and inevitably trusted to become action as in Heine. He introduces Kant by reiterating this conviction that permitted him to regard poets and thinkers as preeminent among revolutionaries:

> Thought strives to become action, the word to become flesh, and marvelous to relate, man like God in the Bible, needs only to express his thought and the world takes form; there is light or darkness; the waters separate themselves from dry land; or it may even be that wild beasts are brought forth. The world is the sign-manual of the word.

So dramatic is the historical rupture brought about by Kant that Heine describes the active forces and the effect of Kant's thought by saying that it will far outstrip the terror of events in the French Revolution. Kant is called the Robespierre of this philosophic revolution, but even such a comparison is inadequate since Kant, who killed a God, far surpassed the destructive force of Robespierre, who only killed a king. Heine introduces Kant by reveling in the irony of the contrast between Kant's violent role in world history and the orderliness, simplicity, and tranquillity of his private life. Like Robespierre, Kant was destined by nature to "weigh out coffee and sugar, but fate decided that they should weigh out other things, and into the scales of the one it laid a king, into the scales of the other a God . . . . And they both gave the correct weight!" Even though Heine rebukes Kant for the act of pity and weakness in the *Critique of Practical Reason* whereby the corpse of the deist God is allowed to reappear in the moral world, he is unstinting in his praise for Kant's achievement in the first critique which

gave birth to a critical spirit that once and for all would prohibit
the return of the great enemy of the future pantheistic harmony — deism.

The key to Kant's achievement is to be found his distinction
between phenomena and noumena which is introduced at the
end of the "Transcendental Analytic" portion of the *Critique of
Pure Reason*. Ultimately this distinction must be seen as resting
upon the earlier distinction between the a priori and a posteriori, as well as upon the analysis of intuition, the intellect, and
the imagination. Heine's purpose, however, is not to retrace the
genesis and justification of this idea, but to explain its basic features and the consequences outlined in the "Transcendental
Dialectic." He rightly reminds the reader that this distinction is
not intended to divide the world of objects into phenomena and
noumena, that is into things that exist and are knowable, and
things that exist and yet are unknowable. Phenomena rather are
objects as they appear, that is things which are found within the
realm described by the conditions of the possibility of the
human experience of knowing; noumena, on the other hand, by
definition do not meet these conditions and so of such things we
can say nothing, neither that they exist or do not exist. The word
noumena serves to remind us of the limits of human knowledge.
Thus we cannot intelligibly or validly speak of what is not of the
phenomenonal world into a transcendent realm; to venture
beyond this world, to risk speaking of the noumenal, is to invite
illusion. Foremost among all that philosophers prior to Kant
once ascribed to this transcendent region is the otherworldly
God. The distant, heavenly God of deism now sits outside of
the legitimate domain of human knowing and speaking, and so
is recognized as a "mere fiction" and the result of a "natural
illusion."

Heine's delight in the death of the deist God should not be
misunderstood as the expression of an atheism on his part. It is

important to bear in mind that it is always only the other-worldly, transcendent, ruler God of deism who need be vanquished in these revolutions. In Heine there is always room, if not the need, for an understanding of the phenomenal world as something divine. If a religion remains in Heine's vision of the future healthy society, then it resembles his understanding of pantheism outlined by Spinoza. While Heine's sense of nature and society lacks a unique Godhead, it never lacks a sense of the divine; though godless he is never without a deep and primitive religious feeling for the holy. His own private relation to religious faith gives an indication that for him the matter of religion was a vexing and never settled one: he was born and raised a Jew, left Judaism and became a harsh critic of religion, but eventually converted to Christianity some years before his death in 1856. These changes in his acceptance of religious doctrine notwithstanding, one could argue that the basic substance of Heine's views on the nature and place of the divine never changed, and that is why he is able to republish this text unaltered but for a new Preface even after his conversion to Christianity.

No one deserves greater merit than Kant in closing the gates upon the unhealthy deist God, yet Heine does not find the German philosophic revolution to be complete with Kant. In the end, Kant lacked the creative genius and poetic vision requisite to such a task. Nevertheless, he did set into motion the final stage of this prelude to the coming political revolution. Now Heine can say that "Germany was drawn into the path of philosophy by Kant, and philosophy became a national cause. A brilliant troop of great thinkers suddenly sprang up on German soil, as if called into being by magical art." History is finally ready for what it has long awaited.

The first successor to Kant is Fichte who, according to Heine, is in no way to be numbered among that brilliant troop of thinkers. While he finds Fichte's position insignificant at best, and, less charitably, "one of the most colossal errors ever hatched in the human brain" Heine nevertheless devotes a large section of the third book largely to heaping scorn and satire upon Fichte's thought and person alike. But Fichte's thought does deserve attention on two accounts: first as playing an important role in the development of the final stage of the German philosophic revolution found in Hegel, and second as once and for all dismissing as misguided the ancient dispute between theism and atheism. Heine, with his own godless sense of the divine, sees the real religious quarrel posed in the deist-pantheist debate, for the question of whether or not there is a divine authority lording over the earth is a question with real social significance. Thought is only squandered when it worries about the existence or non-existence of a God while overlooking the divine and holy quality a nature which properly understood can be the place of "nectar and ambrosia, purple mantles, costly perfumes, luxury and splendor, dances of laughing nymphs, music and comedies." Fichte put his finger on the point when he says that the question of theism is no more important to a philosopher than the question of the color of a triangle is to a mathematician. Likewise Heine finds that the public controversy over charges that Fichte was an athetist provide a clear lesson in the politics of religion. In these matters the case of Fichte is instructive, but in the end his philosophical position has nothing to recommend it to Heine's reading of history, since by his standards it is godless and anti-poetic.

Besides being a misfired attempt to carry on the German tradition after Kant, Fichte's thought actively derailed this historical process. The problem was that he subjectivised the world insofar as the real is only generated out of the ideal, nature out of thought. This is the reason Heine finds Fichte's philosophy godless: Fichte does try to demonstrate the essential harmony of mind and matter, thought and extension, but he does so only by enclosing the real world within the ideal. This collapse of nature into thought represents a retreat rather than an advance to a philosophy that is able to give pantheistic testimony to the divinity of the phenomenal world.

The counterpart and corrective to Fichte is Schelling. By and large Heine judges Schelling to be but an echoer of Fichte since he makes no substantial changes in the Fichtean framework. The simple trade off that is made moving from Fichte to Schelling is clear: while Schelling had a poetic sense absent in Fichte, he lacked Fichte's penetrating dialectical instincts. But Schelling's contribution required neither poetry nor dialectical acumen, for his achievement is simply to have reversed the process outlined by Fichte; rather than simply generating the real from the ideal, he demonstrated how the real becomes the ideal by an equally important process. In Schelling the essential unity of thought and nature is preserved, but not at the one sided price of Fichtean subjectivization. Nature becomes thought in the same process that lets thought become nature; Schelling describes the first process in his *Philosophy of Nature*, while the second is outlined in the *System of Transcendental Idealism*. In this way Schelling complements and reverses the counterrevolutionary tendencies in Fichte's position, and so represents a course correction on the philosophical route to the coming political revolution. The revolutionary tradition inaugurated three centuries earlier by Luther has, in the first decades of Heine's own nineteenth century, matured and so is ripe for its fulfillment.

Hegel represents the last stage and completion of this theoretical odyssey of a culture en route to political revolution and a more harmonious social world. Now Heine can announce that "our philosophical revolution is concluded; Hegel has closed its great circle. Henceforth we see only the developing and perfecting of the philosophy of nature."

Little is said here to present or explain just what enabled Hegel to perform such a titanic task, and to be "the greatest of philosophers begotten by Germany. . . . [one who] far overtops Kant." One likely reason for the relative silence about just what accounts for Hegel's greatness is that Heine regards his own project in this text as in large measure an exercise in Hegelian thought as he understands it. Indeed the parallels between the sense of history and its philosophical underpinnings found in Hegel and Heine are striking. There is a deep kinship between Hegel's account of the parousia of Spirit and Heine's pantheistic vision of nature and society, and of course Hegel's critique of the bad infinite is easy to see as sharing the same intentions as Heine's attack on deism. Furthermore, both agree that the truth of religion is ultimately sublated into the higher form of philosophy. The sense of history operative in each is of a progressive march towards the practical realization of a previously hidden theoretical truth, and in both history is a dialectical process. Finally, both share an especially deep admiration for Luther and Spinoza, along with an equally deep, but qualified, admiration for Kant.

There are many more similarities between them. But the strong Hegelian flavor of Heine's sense of history does not mean that he is merely an epigone. There are significant shifts of emphasis distinguishing them such as the highlighted and unsurmounted roles that language and art play in Heine's conception of culture as opposed to Hegel's. More importantly, the unmitigated revolutionary accent running through Heine's sense of history and society always seems to set him apart from Hegel. The history that one reads in this text is to be understood as a prelude wherein the leitmotives of the coming political revolution are first evident. That is what Heine means when he concludes his discussion of German philosophy by saying that "these doctrines served to develop revolutionary forces that only await their time to break forth and to fill the world with terror and with admiration," and lest we unduly limit the range of these forces, Heine reminds us that "German philosophy is an important fact; it concerns the whole human race." This last remark should not be taken as the expression of an excessive national pride on Heine's part. Heine, who was widely traveled and who wrote this remark while living in Paris as an expatriate, was too cosmopolitan for such cultural myopia. That this text is not a hymn to German culture becomes evident when Germany becomes the target for Heine's wit and satire, especially when it is a matter of the teutonic brutishness and lack of grace in German culture. But Heine does find that the speculative instinct is strongest in German language and culture and that this has given it a leading role in the theoretical development of these world historical revolutionary forces.

Heine never spoke unambiguously about the coming political revolution. His vision of what society should be like and the direction in which history is moving is quite clear and certainly does not lack utopian content and qualities. Yet with all of his confidence in the bond uniting theory and praxis he remained unsure of the real shape that the religious and philosophical revolutions would eventually take; in the end, his teleological sense is too thin for him to say with confidence whether the outcome of these revolutions will deserve praise or blame. Much ink has been spilled in the effort to argue the view that Heine is a prophet of the coming horrors of the National Socialist revolution. It seems almost natural to draw a comparison between the description of the "German thunder" in the last pages here and the events of a century later. But while he was clearly a poet and philosopher, Heine does not necessarily qualify as a prophet nor is it likely that he wished this final celebrated passage to be read as prophecy. It is more likely, more in the spirit of Heine, that the conclusion of this text be read as a declaration of hope as well as of fear. Heine, like Hegel, believed that history had reached a fullness and would soon have to take on a new shape, in looking ahead to the next revolution his utopian hopes were always tempered by his highly developed sense of tragedy and irony. Part of the original contribution of this text is that it serves as a reminder that risk and promise go hand in hand. Both lay ahead, but not just in Heine's day.

There are many reasons why Heine's history of German thought refuses to be outmoded. Here we find a broad and synthetic view of what is at stake in the modern world, and while many of the ideas and events of the past one hundred and fifty years would surely have a retroactive influence upon the history we read here, there is no reason to ask for a modification of his progressive, humanist ideals. Heine believed that theory and practice were both at their best in the service of real human emancipation, and his hope is that when we look to the past we see this has in fact been the case.

Few would dispute the claim that Heine now belongs to the same pantheon of letters and intellectual history that he describes here. His influence was especially strong in the formation of Marx's early critique of religion which Marx worked out when he and Heine knew each other while both were living in Paris. In reading Heine one also finds an anticipation of much in Nietzsche, another who found in Heine an intellectual ancestor. But it is not simply Heine's legacy which recommends him to us today; it is rather in his original contribution to the questions concerning the divine, society, and language that he raises living issues yet to be decided.

TRANSLATOR'S NOTE.

———◆———

In the beginning of the year 1833, Heine contributed to the newly-founded and short-lived Parisian journal, "Europe Littéraire," a series of articles on modern German literature. The object of these articles was to assist French-men to a more accurate acquaintance with the productions of the German Romantic School than it was possible for them to acquire from Madame de Staël's celebrated book, "De l'Allemagne." Political topics being excluded from the programme of the "Europe Littéraire," it was only in a very guarded manner that Heine could, in the pages of this Journal, direct the shafts of his satire against the despotic rulers of Germany. But in the series of three articles published in 1834 in the "Revue des Deux Mondes," and afterwards collected together under the title, "A Contribution to the History of Religion and Philosophy in Germany," Heine felt himself at liberty to deal in the most unrestrained manner with the political condition of his native country. When, however, in January 1835, Hoffmann and Campe of Hamburg published the German version of the work, the mutilation it had suffered at the hands of the censor was so great as to call forth from Heine a protest in the German press. How keenly he resented the treatment to which his work had been submitted will be seen from the Preface to the second German edition (page 10 of the present volume). In the French version of Heine's works, the book now translated appears as the first part of the two volumes entitled "De l'Allemagne." These volumes were carefully revised by Heine during the latter years of his life, but the later German editions had not the benefit of such revision. The French version, as finally revised by the author, must therefore be regarded as the definitive form in which he desired the work to appear. The translator of this volume has therefore been confronted with the difficulty of a French and a German version, presenting considerable variations of text. Some of these variations are so slight as to render it unnecessary to draw special attention to them; indeed to indicate every little change of phrase would prove an annoyance to any but devoted students of Heine's works. Other alterations consist of corrections of errors, a few short passages are materially changed, and several paragraphs appearing in the one version are omitted in the other. Where the alteration in the text seems of importance it is indicated in this volume either by a footnote or in the Appendix, and passages omitted from either version are restored. The actual translation, however, has been made rather from the German than from the French. And for this reason:

it is doubtful whether Heine, wonderful though his mastery of the French language was, wrote the French text without receiving at least partial assistance from some eminent French writer. It certainly was his practice, when preparing French translations of his works which had previously been published in German, to obtain such assistance. It is very probable indeed that the present work also was first written in German, and then rewritten in French for the pages of the "Revue des Deux Mondes." The method of translation here adopted seems therefore to be fully warranted by the circumstances under which the original was composed.

The somewhat cumbrous title in the German version, "Zur Geschichte der Religion und Philosophie in Deutschland," is altered on the title-page of this translation in accordance with the remark of Heine, that the book "is and must remain a fragment." The translator has scrupulously refrained from taking any liberties with the language of his author. Only in a single case has he felt himself compelled to omit a few lines, and in this case the passage omitted is not Heine's own, but a quotation.

The interest in Heine's prose works may now be said to be awakened in this country; thanks in the first place to Matthew Arnold's just and graceful tribute in "Essays in Criticism," and next to the writers of various magazine articles which have of late appeared in England and in America. Mention must specially be made of a recent admirable contribution towards an enlightened estimate of Heine's work, by Mr. Charles Grant in the "Contemporary Review" (September 1880).

It is proper to state that a number of selected passages from "Religion and Philosophy in Germany," appeared in the translator's previous volume, "Heine's Wit, Wisdom, and Pathos." It was the reception accorded to that volume of extracts that induced the translator to undertake the present work.

J. S.

March 1882.

PREFACE

TO THE FIRST FRENCH EDITION.

———◆———

WHEN the Emperor Otho III. visited the tomb in which had reposed for many years the mortal remains of Charlemagne, he entered the vault accompanied by two bishops and by the Count de Laumel, the narrator of these details. The body was not lying stretched out like the other dead, but was seated erect on a bench like a living person. There was a crown of gold on the head and a sceptre was held between the hands, which were gloved; but the nails having grown, had pierced through the leather of the gloves. The vault had been solidly walled round with marble and limestone. In order to obtain access, it was necessary to make a breach in the wall. A very strong odour was perceptible at the moment of entering the tomb. Every one quickly bent the knee and testified his respect for the dead. Otho invested the body of the emperor with a white robe, cut the nails, and repaired whatever had become dilapidated. No portion of the body had suffered decomposition, with the exception of the nose, the point of which was broken off. Otho replaced it with a golden point: he then took from the mouth of the illustrious dead a tooth, caused the wall of the vault to be built up again, and departed. The following night Charlemagne, it is said, appeared to him in a dream, and announced that he, Otho, had not long to live, and that he should leave no heirs.

Such is the story told in the " German Traditions;" but it is not the only story of its kind. It was thus that your King Francis I. caused the tomb of the celebrated Roland to be opened, that he might judge for himself whether this hero had been as great as poets would have us believe. This took place shortly before the battle of Pavia. A like visit was paid by King Sebastian of Portugal to the tombs of his ancestors before embarking for that disastrous African campaign, in which the sands of Alcanzar-Kebir became his shroud. He caused each coffin to be opened, and examined minutely the features of the ancient kings.

Strange and horrible curiosity that often urges men to gaze into the tombs of the past! This curiosity is excited at certain extraordinary periods, at the close of an epoch, or immediately before a catastrophe. We have in our time beheld a similar phenomenon: this was when a great sovereign, the French People, took a fancy, one fine morning, to open the tomb of the past, and to examine by the light of day ages long since dead and forgotten. Skilful gravediggers were not wanting, who set to work with shovel and mattock to remove the rubbish and to make a breach in the vaults. A strong odour was perceptible, a Gothic richness of savour that affected very agreeably noses satiated with classical perfumes. French authors knelt down respectfully before the exhumed Middle Ages. One covered the body with a new cloak, another dressed its nails, a third repaired the nose; after these came several poets, who extracted teeth, just as had been done by the Emperor Otho.

Did the ghost of the Middle Ages appear in a dream to these extractors of teeth and restorers of noses? Did it prophesy to them the speedy end of their Romantic sovereignty? Of this I am ignorant. My chief purpose in speaking of this event in French literature is merely to declare that I have no intention of cavilling at it directly or indirectly when I speak in this book, somewhat harshly, of a similar occurrence that took place in Germany. The German authors who sought to reanimate the Middle Ages had, as will be seen in these pages, another object in view; and the effect produced by them on the great body of the people served to compromise the liberty and the happiness of my country. But in all their efforts, French authors were concerned only about artistic interests, and the French public merely desired to gratify its curiosity. The great majority came to gaze into the sepulchre of the past with no more serious intention than of seeking for an interesting carnival costume. The Gothic mode was, in France, merely a mode that served but to heighten the delights of the present time. Its followers wore their hair flowing in long Middle Age curls; yet a passing remark of the hairdresser to the effect that the mode was unbecoming, was all that was necessary to cause them to cut off by the same snip of the scissors the curled locks of the Middle Ages and the ideas that were attached to them. Alas! it was quite another affair in Germany. The reason of this was, that there the Middle Ages were not utterly dead and decomposed as with you. The German Middle Age period does not lie in its tomb a mere rotten thing; it is often animated by a wicked phantom; it appears amongst us in the full light of day, and sucks the reddest life-blood from our hearts.

Alas! see you not how pale and sad is Germany, and with her all our German youth, but lately so joyously enthusiastic? See you not the blood on the lips of the vampire plenipotentiary, whose residence is at Frankfort, where he sucks with such horrible and wearisome patience at the heart of the German people?

What I have said of the Middle Ages also applies quite specially to the religion of this epoch. The sense of probity demands that I should, as accurately as possible, distinguish the party called Catholic in France from the rogues that bear the same name in Germany. It is only of the latter I have spoken in this book, and in terms, indeed, that appear to me to be far too mild. These are the enemies of my country,—reptiles full of insolent hypocrisy and of incurable baseness. They are to be heard hissing at Berlin as at Munich; and whilst you are tranquilly strolling along the Boulevard Montmartre, you may suddenly feel their sting in your heel. But we shall bruise the head of the old serpent. Its emissaries are the militia of falsehood, they are the familiars of the Holy Alliance, the restorers of all the miseries, of all the horrors, of all the follies of the past.

What an immense distance separates them from the men of the Catholic party in this country, men whose leaders rank amongst the most remarkable writers in France! Though they may not be our brethren in arms, they are fighting on behalf of the same interests as ourselves, the interests of humanity. By this common bond of affection we are united: we are separated only on the question as to what best serves the cause of humanity. They, for their part, believe that humanity has need only of spiritual consolation; whilst we, on the contrary, for

our part, hold that corporeal satisfaction is above all
things necessary for humanity. When the French Catholic party, ignoring its real mission, proclaims itself
the party of the past, the restorer of the faith of the
old time, it becomes our duty to protect it against its
own assertions. The eighteenth century had so completely destroyed Catholicism in France as to leave it with
hardly a sign of life, so that whoever seeks to re-establish
Catholicism amongst you has the aspect of one preaching
an entirely new religion. By France I mean Paris and
not the provinces; for what the provinces think is of as
little consequence as what one's legs think. It is the
head that is the seat of our thoughts. I have been told
that the French of the provinces are good Catholics: I can
neither affirm nor deny it. The men of the provinces
with whom I have conversed have impressed me like
milestones, bearing inscribed on their foreheads the distance, more or less great, from the capital. The women
of the provinces try perhaps to find in Catholicism a consolation for their grief at not being able to live in Paris.
In Paris itself Catholicism ceased in fact to exist at the
Revolution, and long previous to that event it had lost
all real importance. It still lay in wait in the recesses of
the Churches, crouching like a spider in its web, ready to
spring precipitately from its retreat whenever it had a
chance of seizing a child in its cradle, or an old man in his
coffin. It was only at these two periods of life, on arriving in the world and on quitting it, that a Frenchman fell
into the hands of the Christian priest. During all the
intermediate period of his existence he was the servant of
reason, and laughed at holy water and consecrated oil.
Could this then, I ask, be called the reign of Catholicism?

It is because Catholicism was completely extinct in France that it had the power, under Louis XVIII. and Charles X., of attracting to itself, by the charm of novelty, a few disinterested spirits. Catholicism then appeared as something so unheard of, so new, so unexpected! Previous to this period the paramount religion in France was the classical mythology, and this beautiful religion had been so successfully preached to the French people by its authors, its poets, and its artists, that at the close of the preceding century the social and intellectual life of France wore a completely pagan costume. During the Revolution the classical religion flourished in its most vigorous splendour. This was no mere aping of the original after the manner of the Greek Alexandrians. Paris presented the aspect of a natural continuation of Athens and of Rome. Under the empire this antique spirit became insensibly extinguished; the gods of Greece no longer held sway except on the stage, and Roman virtue was in possession only of the battlefield. A new faith had sprung up, a faith summed up in the single name, Napoleon! This faith still rules the masses. It is an error, then, to say that the French people is irreligious because it no longer believes in Christ and his saints; say rather, the irreligion of the French consists, nowadays, in believing in a man, instead of believing in the immortal gods. Say further, the French are irreligious because they have ceased to believe in Jupiter, in Diana, in Minerva, in Venus. The assertion as to Venus may be disputed; at least I know that, as regards the Graces, France has always remained orthodox.

I hope these observations will not be misinterpreted. Their aim is to warn the reader against grievous misconceptions. In the first three parts of this book I have spoken with some detail of the conflicts between religion and philosophy in Germany. It was necessary to explain this intellectual revolution in my country, about which Madame de Staël has spread abroad in France so many erroneous ideas. I frankly admit that I have constantly had in view the work of this grandmother of doctrinaires, and it is with the intention of making reparation that I have given to my book the same title; " On Germany." *

PARIS, 8th *April*, 1833.

---

* This preface appears in the French version of Heine's works, prefixed to the two volumes bearing the title " De l'Allemagne," of which, what is called in the German version " Religion and Philosophy in Germany," forms the first part. It does not appear in any German edition. Its interest, however, is not lessened by that circumstance, and it is the natural introduction to the fragment now presented to the English reader. It also throws light on Heine's second German preface. The dates of the prefaces are themselves significant : 1833, when Heine was in the full vigour of early manhood, and 1852, when he had already lain for several years on his " mattress-grave."—TR.

PREFACE

TO THE FIRST GERMAN EDITION.

———•———

I MUST draw the special attention of German readers to the circumstance that these pages were originally contributed to a French journal, the *Revue des deux Mondes*, and that they were composed with a distinctly temporary object in view. They, in fact, form part of a general survey of intellectual events in Germany, whereof I had already presented a portion to the French public, and this had likewise appeared in German as " A Contribution to the History of Polite Literature in Germany." The exigencies of the periodical press, its defective organisation, the absence of scientific appliances, the inadequateness of French expedients, a newly promulgated law with regard to works printed abroad — a law whose application is found to be limited to myself—these and other obstacles have hindered me from presenting the various parts of my survey in chronological order and under a general title. The present volume therefore, despite its aspect of internal unity and of external completeness, is but the fragment of a greater whole.

I greet my native country with the friendliest of greetings.

Written at Paris,
in the month of December, 1834.

PREFACE

TO THE SECOND GERMAN EDITION.

———•———

WHEN the first edition of this book was published, on taking up a copy of it I was not a little horrified at the mutilation it had suffered, a mutilation of which traces were everywhere visible. Here an adjective was wanting, there a parenthesis, entire passages were omitted regardless of the context, so that not only the meaning, but frequently the intention of the writer, was lost. It was much more the fear of Cæsar than the fear of God that directed the mutilating hand; and whilst all that was insidious from a political point of view was anxiously cast aside, statements the most suspicious regarding religion were permitted to stand. Thus the real tendency of the book—a patriotic democratic tendency—had vanished, and there stared at me from its pages, like an unholy thing, quite a strange apparition that recalled scholastic theological polemics, and that was deeply offensive to the humanistic toleration of my disposition. At first I flattered myself with the hope that in a second impression I should be able to fill up the gaps in the book; but no restoration of this kind is now possible, as the original manuscript disappeared from the house of my publisher during the great fire in

Hamburg.* My memory is too weak to afford me assistance through an effort of recollection ; and besides, on account of the state of my eyes, any minute revision of the book is impossible. I therefore content myself with re-translating from the French version, published before the German version, several of the longer passages omitted, and with intercalating them here. One of these passages, which has been reprinted in innumerable French journals, which has been debated about, and which was even discussed in last year's session of the Chamber of Deputies by one of the greatest of French statesmen, Count Molé, is to be found at the end of this new edition. It may serve to show the true state of the case as to the detraction and degradation of Germany in the eyes of other nations, for which, as certain worthy people asserted, I had been to blame. When, in the sadness of my soul, I gave vent to my feelings regarding the old official Germany, that musty land of Philistines—though it brought forth no Goliath, no, not one great man—there were those that knew how to represent me as speaking of the actual Germany, of the great, mysterious, as it may be called, anonymous Germany of the German people, the sleeping sovereign with whose crown and sceptre the apes are at play. This insinuation of the worthy folk found the readier acceptance, as it was absolutely impossible for me, during a long period, to make any declaration of my real opinion. Particularly was this the case at the time when the decrees of the Germanic Confederacy against " Young

---

* The conflagration of 1842. The manuscript, was however, subsequently recovered, and Dr. Strodtmann made use of it in preparing the complete German edition of Heine's works, published by Hoffmann and Campe, Hamburg.—Tr.

Germany" appeared — decrees directed mainly against myself—which brought me into an exceptional condition of restraint such as had been hitherto unheard of in the annals of press bondage. When, by-and-by, I was at liberty to loosen the muzzle a little, my thoughts still remained gagged.

The book now before the reader is and must remain a fragment. To confess frankly, I had rather that I could leave the book altogether unpublished. And for this reason, that since its first appearance my views on many subjects, especially with regard to sacred things, have undergone important change, and much that was then asserted is now opposed to my better convictions. But the arrow ceases to belong to the archer as soon as it speeds from the string of his bow, and the word ceases to belong to the speaker as soon as it springs from his lips and is multiplied by the press. Besides, I should, by leaving this book unpublished, and by withdrawing it from the complete series of my works, incur the opposition of those having urgent claims upon me. I might, it is true, as is customary with authors in such cases, have recourse to the expedient of toning down expressions, of throwing a veil of phrases over my thoughts; but, from the depth of my soul I abhor all equivocal language, hypocritical flowers of speech, cowardly fig-leaves. Yet, to an honourable man, there remains under all circumstances the inalienable right of openly acknowledging his error — a right that I shall here fearlessly exercise. I therefore candidly confess that everything contained in this book having reference to the great question of the existence of God is as false as it is unadvised. As unadvised and as false is also the assertion, mimicked from the schools, that Deism is in theory destroyed, and that it now only drags out a miserable existence in the material world. No, it is not true that the *Critique of Reason*, which has destroyed the arguments for the existence of God, familiar to mankind since the time of Anselm of Canterbury, has likewise made an end of God himself. Deism lives, lives its most living life; it is not dead, and least of all has it been killed by the newest German philosophy. This fine-spun Berlin dialectic is incapable of enticing a dog from the fireside, it has not power to kill a cat, how much less a God. I have in my own body had experience how slight is the danger of its killing; it is continually at its work of killing, and yet folk remain alive. The doorkeeper of the Hegelian school, the grim Ruge, once obstinately maintained that he had slain me with his porter's staff in the *Halle Chronicle*, though at that very time I was strolling along the boulevards of Paris, healthy and gay, and more unlike dying than ever. Poor worthy Ruge! He himself, at a later period, could not restrain the most honest outburst of laughter when I made him the confession, here, in Paris, that I had never so much as seen that terribly homicidal journal, the *Halle Chronicle;* and my full ruddy cheeks, as well as the hearty appetite with which I swallowed oysters, convinced him how little like a corpse I looked. In fact, in those days I was still healthy and sleek, I stood in the zenith of my fat, and was as arrogant as Nebuchadnezzar before his fall.

Alas! a few years later, a physical and mental change began to take place. How often since those days have I thought of the history of the Babylonian king, who esteemed himself as no less than God, but who, having miserably fallen from the summit of his infatuation, crawled like an animal on the ground eating grass— which would no doubt be salad! This story is to be found in the grandiose and splendid book of Daniel, a story which I recommend to the edifying contemplation, not only of the worthy Ruge, but to that of my far more unregenerate friends, these godless self-gods, Feuerbach, Daumer, Bruno Bauer, Hengstenberg, and whatever else be their names. Besides this one, there are indeed many other beautiful and noteworthy narratives in the Bible which would be worthy their attention, as, for example, just at the beginning, there is the story of the forbidden tree in Paradise and of the serpent, that little private tutoress who lectured on Hegelian philosophy six thousand years before Hegel's birth. This blue-stocking without feet demonstrated very ingeniously how the absolute consists in the identity of being and knowing, how man becomes God through cognition, or, what is the same thing, how the God in man thereby attains self-consciousness. This formula is not so clear as the original words: When ye eat of the tree of knowledge ye shall be as God! Mother Eve understood only one thing in the whole demonstration, that the fruit was forbidden, and because it was forbidden, the good woman ate of it. But she had scarcely eaten the enticing apple when she lost her innocence, her naïve ingenuousness, and discovered that she was much too naked for a person of her position, the ancestress of so many future emperors and kings, and she desired a dress. Truly but a dress of fig-leaves, because in her day no Lyonese silk manufacturers had yet come into the world, and because there were in Paradise no milliners and dressmakers. O Paradise! Strange, as soon as woman attains reasoning self-consciousness, her first thought is of a new dress! And this same Biblical narrative, particularly the saying of the serpent, keeps running in my mind, so that I should like to place it at the beginning of my book by way of motto, in the same manner as one often sees at the gates of princely gardens a board with the warning inscription: Here are man-traps and spring-guns.

In my latest book, " Romancero," I have explained the transformation that took place within me regarding sacred things. Since its publication many inquiries have been made, with zealous importunity, as to the manner in which the true light dawned upon me. Pious souls, thirsting after a miracle, have desired to know whether, like Saul on the way to Damascus, I had seen a light from heaven; or whether, like Balaam, the son of Beor, I was riding on a restive ass, that suddenly opened its mouth and began to speak as a man? No; ye credulous believers, I never journeyed to Damascus, nor do I know anything about it, save that lately the Jews there were accused of devouring aged monks of St. Francis; and I might never have known even the name of the city had I not read the Song of Solomon, wherein the wise king compares the nose of his beloved to a tower that looketh towards Damascus. Nor have I ever seen an ass, at least any four-footed one, that spake as a man, though I have often enough met men who, whenever they opened their mouths, spake as asses. In truth, it was neither a vision, nor a seraphic revelation, nor a voice from heaven, nor any strange dream or other mystery that brought me into the way of salvation; and I owe my conversion simply to the reading of a book. A book? Yes, and it is an old, homely-looking book, modest as nature and natural as it; a book that has a work-a-day and unassuming look, like the sun that warms us, like the bread that nourishes us; a book that seems to us as familiar and as full of kindly blessing as the old grandmother who reads daily in it with dear, trembling lips, and with spectacles on her nose. And this book is called quite shortly—the Book, the Bible. Rightly do men also call it the Holy Scripture; for he that has lost his God can find Him again in this Book, and towards him that has never known God it sends forth the breath of the Divine Word. The Jews, who appreciate the value of precious things, knew right well what they did when, at the burning of the second temple, they left to their fate the gold and silver implements of sacrifice, the candlesticks and lamps, even the breastplate of the High Priest adorned with great jewels, but saved the Bible. This was the real treasure of the Temple, and, thanks be to God! it was not left a prey to the flames or to the fury of Titus Vespasian, the wretch who, as the Rabbin tells us, met with so dreadful a death. A Jewish priest, who lived at Jerusalem two hundred years before the burning of the second temple, during the splendid era of Ptolemy Philadelphus, and who was called Joshua ben Siras ben Eliezer, has written down for us, in a collection of apophthegms, or *Meschalim*, the thoughts of his time about the Bible, and I will here impart to you his beautiful words. There is in them a sacerdotal solemnity, and yet they are as refreshing as if they had but yesterday welled forth from a living human breast; and the words are as follows:—

" All this is the Book of the Covenant made with the Most High God, namely, the Law that Moses commanded as a precious treasure to the house of Jacob. Wisdom floweth therefrom as the water of Pison when it is great, and as the water of Tigris when it overspreadeth its banks in spring. Instruction floweth from it as the Euphrates when it is great, and as Jordan in the harvest. Correction breaketh forth from it as the light, and as the water of the Nile in autumn. There is none that hath ever made an end of learning it, there is none that will ever find out all its mystery. For its wisdom is richer than any sea, and its word deeper than any abyss."

Written at Paris,
in the month of May, 1852.

RELIGION AND PHILOSOPHY
IN GERMANY.

PART FIRST.

———

AFTER labouring for a long time at the work of making France understood in Germany, at the work of destroying those national prejudices that despots so well know how to turn to their account, I am about to undertake a similar and not less useful labour in interpreting Germany to Frenchmen.

Providence, in appointing me this task, will also bestow on me the needful light to perform it. I shall accomplish a work profitable for both countries, and I have entire faith in my mission.

Formerly there prevailed in France the most complete ignorance regarding the intellectual condition of Germany, an ignorance that was most disastrous in times of war. Nowadays, on the other hand, there is springing up a kind of half-knowledge, an erroneous conception of the genius of the German nation, a confusion of old Teutonic doctrines, ominous and most dangerous in times of peace.

Most Frenchmen had persuaded themselves that, in order to comprehend German thought, an acquaintance with the masterpieces of German art was sufficient. But art represents only one side of German thought, and to understand even this requires a knowledge of the other two sides of that thought—Religion and Philosophy.

Only by studying the history of the religious reform proclaimed by Luther, is it possible to comprehend how philosophy reached its development among us, and only by means of a systematic exposition of our philosophical systems can you appreciate that great literary revolution, which, commencing with a theory, with the principles of a new method of criticism, produced the Romanticism that has become the theme of your admiration. You have been admiring flowers about whose roots you knew as little as about the meaning of their symbolical language. You have only seen the colours; you have only breathed the perfumes.

In order then to unveil German thought I must first speak of religion. This religion is Christianity.[1]

Fear not, pious souls! your ears will be offended by no profane pleasantries. These may still be of some service in Germany, where perhaps it is necessary to neutralise, for the moment, the influence of religion. For we Germans are in the same position that you were in previous to the Revolution, when Christianity was inseparably allied to the old order of things. The latter was indestructible so long as the former continued to exercise its influence over the masses. Voltaire's keen laughter must be heard before Samson could strike with the headsman's axe. Yet Voltaire's laugh proved nothing; it produced only a brutal effect, just as did Samson's base axe. Voltaire could only wound the body of Christianity. All his sarcasms derived from ecclesiastical history; all his witticisms on dogma and worship, on the Bible, that most sacred book of humanity, on the Virgin Mary, that fairest flower of poetry; the whole dictionary of philosophical arrows which he discharged against the clergy and the priesthood, could only wound the mortal body of Christianity, but were powerless against its interior essence, its deeper spirit, its immortal soul.

[1] The small figures throughout the work refer to the Notes in the Appendix.

For Christianity is an idea, and as such it is indestructible and eternal, as all ideas are. What then is this idea ?

It is because this idea has not yet been clearly comprehended, because the external forms it has assumed have been taken for the reality, that we are still without a history of Christianity. Although Church history has been written by two opposing parties that are perpetually contradicting each other, yet these parties are so far of one mind, that neither the one nor the other will distinctly declare wherein, after all, consists this idea that is the central point of Christianity; this idea that strives to reveal itself in the symbolism, the dogma, and the worship of the Christian Church, and that has manifested itself in the actual life of Christian peoples. Neither Baronius, the Catholic cardinal, nor Schröckh, the Protestant aulic counsellor, approaches this idea. Though you were to run over the whole collection of the Acts of the Councils, the Code of the Liturgy, and the entire Ecclesiastical History of Sacarelli, you would gain no insight into what constitutes the idea of Christianity. What then do we find in the so-called histories of the Eastern and Western Churches ? In the former nothing but dogmatic subtilties, a revival of the old Greek sophistry ; in the latter mere questions of discipline and disputes concerning ecclesiastical interests, in which the legal casuistry and statecraft of the ancient Romans endeavour to reassert themselves by the aid of new forms and coercive measures. In fact, as men had disputed at Constantinople about the *logos*, so in Rome they contended about the relation between the temporal and the spiritual power: as there they had attacked one another about *homousios*, so here they fought about investiture. But the Byzantine questions—Whether the *logos* is *homousios* to God the Father ? Whether Mary is to be called mother of God or mother of man ? Whether

Christ, in the absence of food, suffered hunger, or only hungered because he desired to hunger?—all these questions were in reality based upon court intrigues; and their solution depended on what was secretly passing in the private apartments of the *Palatium Sacrum.* Everything might be traced to the prattling of women and of eunuchs. Under the name of dogma it is a man, and in the man it is a party that is preferred or persecuted. So likewise in the West. Rome always desired to rule; when her legions fell she sent dogmas into the provinces. Every discussion on matters of faith had reference to Roman usurpations; it was a question of consolidating the supremacy of the Bishop of Rome, who was always very tolerant regarding mere articles of faith, but fretted and fumed whenever the rights of the Church were assailed. He did not indulge in much disputation about the persons in Christ, but he was very eager about the consequences of the decretals of Isidore. He centralised his power by canonical law, by installation of bishops, by abasement of the authority of princes, by the establishing of monastic institutions, by celibacy of the priesthood, and so forth. But was this Christianity? Does the idea of Christianity reveal itself to us in reading this kind of history? And again I ask, what is this idea?

We may discover in what manner this idea had already taken historical form, and manifested itself in the world during the first centuries of the Christian era, by surveying, with minds free from prejudices, the history of the Manicheans and the Gnostics. Though the former were branded as heretics and the latter were decried, though both sects were equally condemned by the Church, their influence on dogma still remained; Christian art was developed from their symbolism, and their mode of thought permeated the whole life of Christian peoples. In the ultimate grounds of their beliefs Manicheans did not greatly

differ from Gnostics. The doctrine of the two principles,
good and evil, at conflict with one another, is common to
both. The one sect, the Manicheans, borrowed this
doctrine from the ancient Persian religion, in which
Ormuzd, light, is opposed to Ahriman, darkness. The
other sect, Gnostics properly so called, believed rather in
the pre-existence of the principle of good, and explained
the origin of the principle of evil by emanation, by gene-
ration of *æons*, which deteriorate in proportion as they
remove from their source. According to Cerinthus, the
Creator of our world was by no means the Most High God,
but only an emanation from Him, one of those *æons*, the
veritable *Demiourgos*, that has insensibly degenerated, and
that now stands, as evil principle, in hostile opposition to
the *logos*, the good principle, emanating directly from the
Supreme God. This Gnostic cosmogony is of Indian
origin, and embodies the doctrine of the incarnation of
God, of the mortification of the flesh, of the contemplative
life; it has given birth to asceticism, to monastic abnegation, the purest flower of the Christian idea. This idea
manifested itself, very confusedly however, in dogma, and
very vaguely in worship. Still we find everywhere appearing the doctrine of these two principles; the perverse
Satan is opposed to the good Christ; the spiritual world is
represented by Christ, the material world by the devil;
the soul belongs to the former, the body to the latter.
The whole external world, Nature, is therefore by its origin
wicked, and Satan, the prince of darkness, seeks by its
means, to entice us to destruction; and we must renounce
all the pleasures of the senses, we must torture the body,
the fief of Satan, in order that the soul may soar more
majestically towards the heavenly light, towards the radiant
kingdom of Christ.

This cosmogony, the veritable idea of Christianity, spread
with incredible rapidity throughout the extent of the

Roman empire. It raged like a disease; its sufferings, its fever, its extreme tension continued during the whole of the Middle Ages; and we moderns often feel even yet its spasms and its lassitude in all our members. If some one amongst us has meantime been cured, yet is it impossible for him to escape the all-pervading lazaretto atmosphere, and he feels himself unhappy as the only healthy being amidst the multitude of languishing mortals. One day, when humanity will have regained robust health, when peace will have been once more established between body and soul, and they again live together in primal harmony, it will scarce be possible for men to comprehend the unnatural enmity that Christianity has set between them. Happier and fairer generations, born of free unions, and nurtured in a religion of joy, will smile with pity when thinking of their poor ancestors, whose lives were passed in melancholy abstinence from all the enjoyments of this beautiful world, and who mortified the warm, rosy-hued flesh till they became mere pale, cold ghosts. Yes ! I declare it with full conviction : our descendants will be a fairer and happier race than we are. For I believe in progress; I believe that happiness is the goal of humanity, and I cherish a higher idea of the Divine Being than those pious folk who suppose that man was created only to suffer. Even here on earth I would strive, through the blessings of free political and industrial institutions, to bring about that reign of felicity which, in the opinion of the pious, is to be postponed till heaven is reached after the day of judgment. The one expectation is perhaps as vain as the other; there may be no resurrection of humanity either in a political or in a religious sense. Mankind, it may be, is doomed to eternal misery ; the nations are perhaps under a perpetual curse, condemned to be trodden under foot by despots, to be made the instruments of their accomplices and the laughing-stocks of their menials. Yet, though all this be the case, it will be the duty even of those who regard Christianity as an error still to uphold it; and men must journey barefoot through Europe, wearing monks' cowls, preaching the doctrine of renunciation and the vanity of all earthly possessions, holding up before the gaze of a scourged and despised humanity the consoling Cross, and promising, after death, all the glories of heaven[2].

The duration of religions has always been dependent on human need for them. Christianity has been a blessing for suffering humanity during eighteen centuries; it has been providential, divine, holy. All that it has done in the interest of civilisation, curbing the strong and strengthening the weak, binding together the nations through a common sympathy and a common tongue, and all else that its apologists have urged in its praise—all this is as nothing compared with that great consolation it has bestowed on man. Eternal praise is due to the symbol of that suffering God, the Saviour with the crown of thorns, the crucified Christ, whose blood was as a healing balm that flowed into the wounds of humanity. The poet especially must acknowledge with reverence the terrible sublimity of this symbol. The whole system of symbolism impressed on the art and the life of the Middle Ages must awaken the admiration of poets in all times. In reality, what colossal unity there is in Christian art, especially in its architecture! These Gothic cathedrals, how harmoniously they accord with the worship of which they are the temples, and how the idea of the Church reveals itself in them! Everything about them strives upwards, everything transubstantiates itself; the stone buds forth into branches and foliage, and becomes a tree; the fruit of the vine and the ears of corn become blood and flesh; the man becomes God; God becomes a pure spirit. For the poet, the Christian life of the Middle Ages is a precious and inexhaustibly fruitful field. Only through Christianity could the circumstances of life combine to form such striking contrasts, such motley sorrow, such weird beauty, that one almost fancies such things can never have had any real existence, and that it is all a vast fever-dream— the fever-dream of a delirious deity. Even Nature, during this sublime epoch of the Christian religion, seemed to have put on a fantastic disguise; for oftentimes though man, absorbed in abstract subtilties, turned away from her with abhorrence, she would recall him to her with a voice so mysteriously sweet, so terrible in its tenderness, so powerfully enchanting, that unconsciously he would listen and smile, and become terrified, and even fall sick unto death. The story of the nightingale of Basle comes here into my recollection, and as it is probably unknown to you I will relate it.

One day in May, 1433, at the time of the Council of Basle, a company of clerics, composed of prelates, doctors, monks of every colour, were walking in a wood near the town. They were disputing about points of theological controversy, distinguishing and arguing, contending about annates, expectatives, and reservations, inquiring whether Thomas Aquinas was a greater philosopher than Bonaventura, and so forth. But suddenly, in the midst of their dogmatic and abstract discussions, they all became silent, and remained as if rooted to the spot before a blossoming lime-tree, wherein sat a nightingale carolling and sobbing forth her tenderest and sweetest melodies. These learned men began to feel in a strangely blessed mood as the warm spring notes of the bird penetrated their scholastic and monastic hearts; their sympathies awoke out of their dreary winter sleep, and they looked on one another in raptured amazement. But at last one of them shrewdly remarked that herein must be some wile of the evil one, that this nightingale could be none other than an emissary of the devil, seeking to divert them by its seducing strains from their Christian converse, and to entice them into voluptuousness or other alluring sin, and he thereupon proceeded to exorcise the evil spirit, probably with the customary formula of the time :—*Adjuro te per eum, qui venturus est, judicare vivos et mortuos.* To this adjuration it is said that the bird replied, " Yea, I am an evil spirit," and flew away laughing. They, however, that had listened to its song fell sick that same day, and died shortly thereafter.

This story needs no commentary. It bears the terrible impress of a time when all that was sweet and lovely was decried as the agency of the devil. The nightingale itself was declared a bird of evil fame, and men made the sign of the cross when it sang. The true Christian walked abroad with his sentient being wrapped in anxious reserve, like an abstraction, like a spectre in the midst of smiling nature. I shall perhaps, in a later work, speak more at length of the relation established between the Christian soul and nature ; for in order to elucidate the spirit of modern romantic literature, I shall be obliged to discuss minutely German popular superstitions.* For the present I can only remark that French authors, misled by certain German authorities, have fallen into gross error in supposing that during the Middle Ages popular superstitions were identical throughout the whole of Europe. It was only with regard to the principle of good, the kingdom of Christ, that the same views were universally entertained in Europe. The Church of Rome took care that it should be so, and whoever deviated on this subject from the prescribed opinion was a heretic. But with regard to the principle of evil, the empire of Satan, opinions varied in the various countries. In the Teutonic north, men's con-

* Heine (in part at least) fulfilled this promise in his " Elementary Spirits."—Tr.

ceptions of this principle differed entirely from those held
in the Latin countries of the south.   This difference arose
from the fact that the Christian priesthood did not reject
as idle dreams the old national divinities, but conceded to
them a real existence, asserting however, that all these
deities were but male or female devils, who through the
triumph of Christ had lost their power over men, and were
now seeking to allure them back to sin by wiles and sensual delights.   All Olympus had become an aërial hell;
and if a poet of the Middle Ages celebrated the epos of the
Greek divinities, sang he ever so sweetly, the pious Christian beheld in his song only goblins and demons.   The
dismal anathema of the monks fell most rudely on poor
Venus; she especially was held to be a daughter of Beel-
zebub, and the good knight Tanhäuser tells her even to
her face—

> " O Venus, O thou goddess mine,
>   Thou'rt but a devil fair and fine ! "

For Venus had enticed this knight Tanhäuser into that
wonderful cavern in what is called the Mountain of
Venus, wherein, as the legend tells, the beautiful goddess
and her attendants lead, amidst pastime and dance, the
most dissolute life.   Poor Diana, too, despite her chastity,
was not exempt from a like fate, and was accused of scouring the woods by night with her nymphs; hence the
legends of the fierce huntsman and the wild nightly chase.
Here we have indications of the true Gnostic conception
as to the deterioration of the previously divine, and in this
transformation of ancient national beliefs the idea of Christianity most profoundly manifests itself.

National faith in Europe, though more strongly marked
in the northern than in the southern countries, was pantheistic.   Its mysteries and symbols were referable to a
worship of nature; in every element men adored some
marvellous being, every tree revealed a deity, all the phe-

nomena of the universe were informed by divinity. Christianity reversed this view; nature, ceasing to bear the impress of the divine, became diabolised. But the joyous and artistically beautiful forms of Greek mythology that were still potent side by side with Latin civilisation in the south, could not so readily be transformed into the hideous and repulsive features of Satan as the Teutonic gods, over whose creation certainly no artistic thought had presided, and who were always as dreary and as sad as their northern abodes. Thus in France you could produce no such gloomy and terrible kingdom of Satan as we in Germany, and the world of apparitions and sorcery even assumed with you a genial aspect. How beautiful, how distinct and many-coloured are the popular legends of France compared with those of Germany; those monstrosities of blood and cloud that glare at us with such wan and cruel countenances. Our poets of the Middle Ages, selecting in general such materials as had either been first imagined or first treated in Brittany and Normandy, imparted to their works, perhaps intentionally, as much as possible of the genial old French spirit. But our national poetry and our traditional folk-lore preserved that dismal northern spirit of which you can hardly form any idea. Like us you have many kinds of elementary spirits, but ours differ as widely from yours as a German differs from a Frenchman. How brightly coloured and especially how cleanly are the demons of your *fabliaux* and wizard romances in comparison with the rabble-rout of our colourless and very often filthy ghosts! Your fays and sprites, whether borrowed from Cornwall or from Arabia, become quite naturalised among you, and a French ghost is distinguished from a German ghost much as a dandy wearing kid gloves and dawdling along the Boulevard Coblence is distinguished from a clumsy German porter. Your water sprites, such as Melusine, have as little resemblance to ours as a princess has to a washerwoman.   How horrified your fay Morgana would be did she chance to meet a German witch, naked, smeared with ointment, riding on a broomstick to the Brocken !   This mountain is no fair Avallon, but a meeting-place for all that is abominable and hideous.   On the summit of the mountain sits Satan in the form of a black goat.   Each witch approaches him bearing a lighted candle, and kisses the spot where the back ceases.   Thereafter the whole crazy sisterhood dances round him, singing *donderemus, donderemus !* the goat bleats, the infernal rabble shouts.   It is an evil omen for a witch to lose a shoe in this dance ; it betokens that she will be burnt that same year.   But the mad sabbat-music, worthy of Berlioz, overpowers all foreboding anxiety, and when the poor witch wakes in the morning from her intoxication, it is to find herself lying naked and exhausted among the ashes of the dying fire.

The best information concerning these witches is to be found in the " Demonology " of the honourable and learned Doctor Nicolas Remigius, criminal judge to his serene highness the Duke of Lorraine.   This sagacious man had certainly the best opportunity for becoming acquainted with the doings of the witches, for he conducted the prosecutions against them, and in his time eight hundred women in Lorraine alone were burnt at the stake, after being convicted of witchcraft.   Proof of their guilt was mainly established in this wise : their feet and hands being bound together, they were thrown into the water.   If they sank and were drowned, they were innocent ; but if they remained floating on the surface, they were pronounced guilty, and were burnt.   Such was the logic of the time.

The main feature in the character of German demons is that everything ideal has been stripped from them, and thus they exhibit a mixture of the vile and the horrible.   The more coarsely familiar the form in which they present themselves the more terrible the effect they produce. Nothing can be weirder than our hobgoblins, cobolds, and gnomes. Prætorius, in his *Anthropodemus Plutonicus,* has a passage on this subject which I quote from Dobeneck.*

"The ancients could not conceive hobgoblins (*Poltergeister*) as other than veritable men of the stature of diminutive children wearing parti-coloured little coats or dresses. Some add that they have a knife sticking from their backs, they having been done to death with this instrument; and as thus represented they have a hideous aspect. The superstitious believe them to be the souls of former occupants of their houses, who had been murdered. They tell, also, many a story as to how these cobolds, after rendering good service to the maids and cook-wenches in the house, so won their affections that many of these servants became enamoured of the cobolds to such a degree that they experienced an ardent desire to see the manikins, and eagerly longed for their appearance. But the spirits would never willingly gratify this longing, making the excuse that they could not be seen without inspiring horror. Though, when the maids persisted in their desire to behold them, the cobolds would indicate some part of the house where they would present themselves corporeally. The persons wishing to see the cobolds must, however, bring with them a pail of cold water. Now it sometimes happened that one of these cobolds would lay himself down naked and as if dead on the ground with a long knife sticking in his back. On seeing the creature thus lying, many a servant became so sorely terrified that she would fall down fainting. Thereupon the thing would immediately spring up, seize the water-pail and souse the girl with its contents in order to bring

* Dobeneck's "German Popular Superstitions and Heroic Legends of the Middle Ages."

her to her senses. After this the maid would lose all desire for the creature, and would never again seek to behold little Chim. For you must know the cobolds all have particular names, though generally called *Chim.* It is said also that for the men and maid servants to whom they are devoted they will perform all kinds of house-work: currying and feeding the horses, cleaning the stable, scouring up everything, tending the cows, doing whatever is necessary in and about the house, and paying such attention that the cattle grow fat and sleek under their care. In return the cobolds require to be much indulged by the domestics, who dare not cause them the slightest offence either by laughing at them or by neglect-ing to provide their food. And a cook-wench having taken one of these little creatures into her secret service, must set down for it daily at the same hour and in an appointed place in the house, a dish of well prepared and well seasoned food, and then go her way without looking behind; after that she may pass her time in idleness, and go to bed when she pleases; yet at early morning she will find all her work carefully performed. But should she on a single occasion neglect her duty, as by omitting to set down the food, she will be obliged to do her work without assistance, and will meet with all kinds of mishaps: either getting herself burned with hot water, or breaking the pots and dishes, or spilling the sauce and so forth—misadventures that infallibly bring upon her a scolding from the master or mistress of the house, at which the cobold may often be heard tittering and laughing. And such a cobold is accustomed to remain in a house even though the servants are changed. Indeed, a maid when she is leaving a house ought to recommend the cobold to her successor, so that it may continue its services in the household. Should the new servant pay no heed to the recommendation she will not fail to meet with perpetual misfortunes and will speedily be forced to quit the house."

The following anecdote is perhaps one of the most terrible of its kind.

A maid-servant had during many years an invisible familiar spirit that sat beside her by the hearth, where she had set apart for it a little place, entertaining herself with the creature during the long winter evenings. Now the maid once begged Heinzchen (for so the spirit was called) to show himself to her in his natural form. Heinzchen, however, refused to do so. At last, after much entreaty, he consented, and bade the maid descend into the cellar and there she would see him. The girl, taking a candle, goes down into the cellar, and there in an open cask she beholds a dead infant swimming in its blood. Now this servant had many years before given birth to a child, and had secretly murdered and concealed it in a cask.

Such is the idiosyncrasy of the Germans that they often seek in the horrible their merriest jests, and the popular legends relating to cobolds are frequently characterised by diverting traits. The most amusing of such stories are those about Hüdeken, a cobold that carried on his pranks at Hildesheim in the twelfth century, of whom there is so much talk amongst our gossiping spinsters and in our romances of the spirit-world. I borrow from the Chronicle of the Monastery of Hirschau, by the Abbot Tritheim, the following narrative :—

"In the year 1132 there appeared to many persons in the bishopric of Hildesheim, being seen of them during a considerable time, an evil spirit in the form of a peasant with a hat on his head ; whence the country people called it, in the Saxon language, *Hüdeken* (little hat). This spirit took delight in haunting people, being sometimes visible, sometimes invisible, in asking questions and in replying

to their queries.   He gave offence to no one without cause.
When, however, any one mocked at or otherwise insulted
him, he avenged the injury done him in the completest
manner.   The Count Burchard of Luka having been killed
by the Count Hermann of Weissenburg, and the territory
of the latter being in danger of falling into the hands of
the avengers of the murdered count, Hüdeken awoke the
Bishop of Hildesheim out of sleep, and spoke to him in
these words: 'Arise, bald-head! the county of Weissenburg is abandoned and become vacant through the mur-
derous deed of its seigneur, and thou may'st easily obtain
possession of it.'   The bishop speedily assembled his
men-at-arms, fell upon the land of the guilty count, and
united it, with permission of the emperor, to his bishopric.
The spirit repeatedly and importunately gave warning to
the said bishop of impending dangers, and frequently
appeared in the kitchens of the episcopal palace, where he
conversed with the scullions and rendered them all manner
of service.   The domestics having by degrees become very
familiar with Hüdeken, a young scullion was daring enough
to tease him and even to souse him with dirty water as
often as he made his appearance.   The spirit besought the
chief cook or steward of the kitchens to forbid the imper-
tinent boy's indulgence in such mischief.   To this request
the chief cook answered, 'Thou art a spirit and yet art
thou afraid of a mere boy!'   Whereupon Hüdeken replied
in a menacing tone, 'Since thou wilt not punish the boy,
I shall show thee within a few days how far I am afraid of
him.'   Soon after this it happened that the boy who had
offended the spirit was in the kitchen quite alone and
asleep.   In this condition the spirit seized him, stabbed
him, cut the body in pieces and threw the fragments into
the pots placed over the fire.   When the cook discovered
what had been done, he cursed the spirit; and next day
Hüdeken spoiled all the roasts that were on the spits, by

pouring over them the venom and blood of vipers. The
thirst for revenge suggested to the cook new insults, until
finally the spirit enticed him on to an enchanted false
bridge, thus causing him to fall into the castle moat. After
this Hüdeken made the walls and towers of the town his
nightly haunt, causing much anxiety to the sentinels, and
obliging them to keep a diligent watch. A citizen that
had an unfaithful wife said jestingly, one day as he was
about to set out on a journey, 'Hüdeken, my good friend,
I commend my wife to thy charge; guard her carefully!'
As soon as the husband had gone his faithless wife permitted her lovers, one after another, to visit her. But
Hüdeken did not let a single one of them approach her,
and threw them all out of bed on to the floor. When the
husband returned from his journey, the spirit went to meet
him, and said to him, 'I am heartily glad of thy return,
whereby I am relieved of the burdensome duty thou didst
lay on me. I have with unspeakable difficulty preserved
thy wife from actual disloyalty, and I beg thee never again
to place her under my care. I had rather have the keep-
ing of all the swine in the whole Saxon land than of a
woman that seeks by deceit to throw herself into the arms
of her lovers.'"

I ought, for the sake of historical accuracy, to remark
that the hat worn by Hüdeken differs from the ordinary
costume of cobolds. They are generally clad in grey, and
wear a red cap; at least this is the garb they assume in
Denmark, where nowadays they are to be met with in
greatest numbers. I used to be of opinion that they had
chosen Denmark as their favourite resort from their fond-
ness for red groats. But a young Danish poet, Herr Ander-
sen, whom I had the pleasure of meeting in Paris this
summer, positively assured me that the favourite food of
the *nissen* (as the cobolds are called in Denmark) is fru-
menty with butter. Once these cobolds have taken up

their abode in a house they are not disposed readily to quit it again.   Yet they never come without previous announcement, and when desiring to settle down anywhere they give notice of their intention to the master of the house in the following manner:—They carry into the house by night a great quantity of wood-chips and strew the ordure of cattle in the milk-cans.   If the master of the house does not throw out the wood-chips, if he and his family consume the milk thus made foul, then the cobolds instal themselves permanently in his house.   A poor Jutlander became at last so much annoyed at the enforced companionship of such a cobold, that he determined to abandon his whole house to the creature.   Loading his goods and chattels on a cart, he drove off with them towards the next village, in order to settle there.   But on the way thither, chancing to look round, he espied, peeping out of one of the empty milk-churns, the little red-capped head of the cobold, who called out to him complacently, " *Wi flütten !* " (we are flitting).

I have perhaps lingered too long over these little demons, and it is time that I should return to the great ones.   Yet all these legends illustrate the character and the beliefs of the German people.   These beliefs were formerly just as powerful in influence as was the creed of the Church. By the time the learned doctor Remigius had completed his great work on witchcraft, he believed himself to be so completely master of his subject as to imagine that he could himself exercise the power of sorcery; and, conscientious man that he was, he did not fail to denounce himself to the tribunals as a sorcerer, and was burned as such on the strength of his own testimony.

These atrocities did not originate directly in the Christian Church, though indirectly such was their origin; for, the Church had so cunningly inverted the old Teutonic religion, that the pantheistic cosmogony of the Germans was transformed into a pandemonic conception; the former popular divinities were changed into hideous fiends. But man does not willingly abandon that which has been dear to his forefathers, and his affections secretly cling firmly thereto, even when it has been mutilated and defaced. Hence popular superstitions, travestied as they have become, may in Germany outlive the official creed of our days, which is not, like them, rooted in the ancient nationality. At the time of the Reformation, faith in the Catholic legends disappeared with great rapidity; but not so belief in enchantments and sorcery. Luther ceases to believe in Catholic miracles; but he still believes in the power of the devil. His " Table-Talk " is full of curious anecdotes of Satanic art, of cobolds and witches. He himself, in his distress, often fancies that he is engaged in combat with the devil in person. On the Wartburg, where he translated the New Testament, he was so much disturbed by the devil that he threw the inkstand at his head. The devil has ever since that day had a great dread of ink, and a still greater dread of printing-ink. Of the craftiness of the devil many a diverting anecdote is told in this same book of " Table-Talk;" and I cannot forbear here quoting one of these—

" Dr. Martin Luther related that one day certain boon companions were sitting together in a tavern. Now amongst them was a wild disorderly fellow, who said, were any one to offer him a stoup of good wine, he was ready to sell his soul therefor.

" A little while afterwards there comes into the room one that seats himself beside him that had been so foolhardy, drinks with him, and amidst other talk, says to him—' Listen, said'st thou not but a little ago, if any one should give thee a stoup of wine thou would'st sell him thy soul therefor ? '

"Then said the other—'Yea, and I hold to it; let me drink and carouse and be right merry to-day.'

"The man, who was the devil, said 'Yes,' and soon slipped away again from him. Now when this same drinker had passed the whole day jovially, and had at last become drunk, then the aforesaid man, the devil, returns, seats himself again beside him, and says to the other topers— 'Good sirs, what think you; when one buys a horse, do not saddle and bridle also become his?' They were all taken with great fear. At last the man said, 'Come, tell me without more ado.' Then they all avowed it was so, and said, 'Yea, saddle and bridle also are his.' Whereupon the devil takes hold of that same wild unruly fellow and carries him off through the roof, and no one could tell whither he went."

Although I entertain the highest respect for our great master, Martin Luther, still I cannot but think he has quite mistaken the character of the devil. The devil does not look upon the body with such contempt as is here represented. And, however evil-spoken of the devil may be, he can never be accused of being a spiritualist.

But Martin Luther misjudged the sentiments of the Pope and the Catholic Church even more seriously than he did those of the devil. In my strict impartiality, I must take the two former, as I have taken the devil under my protection, against the all-too-zealous man. In truth, if asked as a matter of conscience, I should admit that Pope Leo X. was in reality far more reasonable than Luther; and that the Reformer had quite misunderstood the fundamental principles of the Catholic Church. For Luther did not perceive that the idea of Christianity, the annihilation of the life of the senses, was too violent a contradiction of human nature ever to be capable of complete realisation. He did not comprehend that Catholicism was a species of concordat between God and the

devil, between spirit and matter, whereby the autocracy
of the spirit was theoretically admitted, whilst matter was
placed in the position of carrying out in practice all its
annulled rights. Hence a subtle system of concessions
devised by the Church for the benefit of the senses, though
so conceived as to stigmatise every act of sensuality and
to preserve to the spirit its arrogant usurpation. Thou
art permitted to lend an ear to the tender emotions of the
heart and to embrace a pretty girl, but thou must acknowledge that it is an abominable sin, and for this sin
thou must do penance. That such penance might take
the form of money payment was as advantageous for
humanity as it was profitable for the Church. The Church
ordained, so to speak, a ransom to be paid for every fleshly
indulgence; and thus was established a tariff for every
species of sin. There were religious pedlars offering for
sale throughout the land, in the name of the Romish
Church, indulgences for every taxable sin. Such a pedlar
was Tetzel, upon whom Luther made his first onslaught.
Our historians hold the opinion that this protest against
the traffic in indulgences was an insignificant event, and
that it was only through Romish obstinacy that Luther
(whose zeal was at first directed merely against an ecclesiastical abuse) was driven to attack the authority of the
Church in its most important position. But this is certainly an error; indulgence-mongering was not an abuse,
it was a consequence of the whole ecclesiastical system,
and in attacking it Luther attacked the Church itself, and
the Church must condemn him as a heretic. Leo X., the
subtle Florentine, the disciple of Politian, the friend of
Raphael, the Greek philosopher with the tiara conferred
on him by the conclave, possibly because he was suffering
from a disease in no wise caused by Christian abstinence,
and which was still very dangerous—how must this Leo
de Medicis have laughed at the poor, chaste, simple monk

who imagined the Gospel to be the charter of Christen-
dom, and that this charter must be a truth! He may
perhaps have quite overlooked what Luther was seeking,
much busied as he then was with the building of St.
Peter's, the cost of which was to be defrayed by this very
sale of indulgences, vice being thus made contributory to
the erection of this edifice, which thereby became a kind
of monument of sensual desire, like the pyramid of Rho-
dope, constructed by an Egyptian courtesan from the
profits of prostitution. Of this house of God it may with
more justice be asserted than of the Cathedral of Cologne,
that it was built by the devil. This triumph of spiritualism, that compelled sensualism to rear for it its fairest
temple; that derived from innumerable concessions
granted to the flesh, the means of glorifying the spirit—
this triumph was a thing incomprehensible in the German
North. For there, more easily than under the glowing
sky of Italy, it was possible to practise a Christianity that
makes the least possible concessions to sensuality. We
Northerners are of colder blood, and we needed not so
many indulgences for carnal sins as were sent by Leo in
his fatherly concern for us. Our climate facilitates the
practice of Christian virtues; and on the 31st October,
1516, as Luther nailed his theses against indulgences to
the door of the Augustin Church, the moat that surrounded Wittenberg was perhaps already frozen over, and
one could have skated on it, which is a very cold sort
of pleasure, and consequently no sin.

I have been making use repeatedly of the words
spiritualism and *sensualism*. I shall explain them later
on when I come to speak of German philosophy. It suf-
fices here to remark that I do not employ these expressions to designate philosophical systems, but merely to
distinguish two social systems of which one, spiritualism,
is based on the principle that it is necessary to annul all

the claims of sense in order to accord exclusive authority
to the spirit; that it is necessary to mortify, to stigmatise,
to crush the flesh that we may the better glorify the soul:
whilst the other system, sensualism, revindicates the rights
of the flesh, which neither ought to be nor can be abrogated.[3]

The beginnings of the Reformation revealed at once
the whole extent of its range. No Frenchman has ever
yet comprehended the significance of this great event.
The most erroneous ideas prevail in France regarding the
Reformation; and I must add that these views will perhaps prevent Frenchmen ever arriving at a just apprecia-
tion of German life.[4] The French understood only the
negative side of the Reformation; they beheld in it merely
a war against Catholicism, and often imagined that the
combat that took place on the opposite side of the Rhine
was waged with the same motives as a similar combat
here in France. But the motives were totally different.
The conflict with Catholicism in Germany was nothing
else than a war begun by spiritualism when it perceived
that it possessed merely the title of authority and ruled
only *de jure*, whilst sensualism by means of a long established system of fraud was exercising actual sovereignty
and was governing *de facto*. The retailers of indulgences
were expelled, the fair concubines of the priests were
replaced by cold legitimate spouses, the alluring images
of the Madonna were dashed to pieces and a Puritanism
utterly hostile to all pleasures of the senses took possession
of the land. The conflict with Catholicism in France
during the seventeenth and eighteenth centuries was, on
the contrary, a war begun by sensualism, when, though
de facto sovereign, it beheld every act of its authority
derided as illegitimate, and reviled in the most cruel
manner by a spiritualism that existed only *de jure*. But
whereas in Germany the battle was waged with chaste
earnestness, in France it was fought with wanton jests,

and whilst yonder men engaged in theological discussions, here they composed merry satires.   Usually the object of these satires was to show the contradiction into which man falls when he seeks to be wholly spiritual: hence delicious stories of pious men succumbing involuntarily to sensual appetites, or striving to save the appearance of sanctity by taking refuge in hypocrisy.   The Queen of Navarre had already portrayed in her novels such perplexities.   Her customary theme is the relation of monks to women, and her aim is not merely to convulse with laughter but to shake the foundations of monasticism. Molière's "Tartuffe" is indisputably the most malicious production of this merry polemic; for this comedy is directed not merely against the Jesuitism of its age but against Catholicism itself, nay, against the idea of Christianity, against spiritualism.   Tartuffe's paraded dread of the naked bosom of Dorine, his language to Elmire:—

> "Le ciel défend, de vrai, certains contentements,
> Mais on trouve avec lui des accommodements :"—

all these things tend to bring into ridicule not only ordinary hypocrisy, but also the universal falsehood that necessarily arises from the impossibility of carrying out the Christian idea, along with the whole system of concessions that spiritualism is forced to make to sensualism. Truly, the Jansenists had far greater cause than the Jesuits for feeling aggrieved at the performance of the comedy of "Tartuffe," and Molière may well be as insupportable to Protestant Methodists of our day as he was to the Catholic devotees of his own time.   It is this that makes Molière so grand; for, like Aristophanes and Cervantes, he ridicules not merely the eccentricities of his contemporaries, but the eternal absurdities and the primal weaknesses of humanity. Voltaire, whose attacks were always upon things temporary and unessential, stands in this respect far below Molière.

But this species of ridicule, the Voltairean, has fulfilled its mission in France, and any attempt to continue it would be both unseasonable and impolitic. For were it sought to extirpate the last visible remnants of Catholicism it might readily happen that the idea of Catholicism would assume a new form, clothe itself with a new body, and laying aside the very name of Christianity might, thus transformed, become more vexatious and oppressive than in its present shattered, ruined, and discredited condition. Yea, it is not without its advantage that spiritualism is represented by a religion that has already lost the better part of its strength, and by a priesthood that is in complete antagonism with the enthusiasm for liberty that characterises our time.

But why then is spiritualism so repugnant to us? Is it so bad a thing? By no means! Attar of roses is a precious thing, and a phial of this essence is refreshing for those that are obliged to wear out their days in the closed chambers of a harem. But we would not that all the roses of this life should be crushed and trampled down in order to obtain a few drops of such essence, however great the solace it might afford. We resemble rather the nightingales that delight in the roses themselves and derive as great an ecstasy from their crimson blossoming as from their ethereal perfume.

I have asserted that the attack upon Catholicism in Germany was delivered by spiritualism. But this applies only to the commencement of the Reformation. As soon as spiritualism had made a breach in the old edifice of the Church, sensualism with all its long restrained fervour of passion threw itself into it, and Germany became the tumultuous arena of combatants intoxicated with liberty and sensual delights. The oppressed peasantry had found in the new doctrine intellectual weapons with which to wage war against the aristocracy; for centuries they had nourished the desire for such a combat. At Münster sensualism, in the person of John of Leyden, ran naked through the streets and laid itself down with its twelve wives in the huge bed, to be seen to this day, in the council house of the town. Everywhere the doors of monasteries flew open, and monks and nuns rushed billing and cooing into each other's arms. In truth the history of Germany at this time consists of little else than sensualistic riots. We shall presently see how small was the result of this reaction, how spiritualism succeeded in overpowering these rioters, how it gradually secured its authority in the north, and how it was mortally wounded by philosophy, the enemy that it had nurtured in its bosom. It is a very complicated history, most difficult to unravel. For the Catholic party it is easy to assign at pleasure the worst motives; and to hear them speak one would suppose that the sole objects were to legitimise the most shameless sensuality and to plunder the goods of the Church. Doubtless in order to obtain the victory intellectual interests must always form an alliance with material interests; but the devil had so oddly shuffled the cards that it is now impossible to affirm with certainty anything about intentions.

The illustrious personages who, on the 17th of April, 1521, were assembled in the Diet Hall at Worms might well cherish in their hearts many a thought at variance with the words on their lips. *There* sat a young Emperor, who, as he wrapped himself with the ecstasy of youthful sovereignty in the folds of his new purple mantle, secretly rejoiced that the proud Roman Pontiff who had so often dealt hardly with his imperial predecessors, nor had even yet resigned his arrogant pretensions, was about to receive a most effectual reprimand. The representative of the proud Roman had, on his side, ground for secret joy that disunion had betrayed itself amongst those Germans, who,

like drunken barbarians, had so often invaded and plun-
dered fair Italy, and still threatened her with new inva-
sions and plunderings. The temporal princes rejoiced that,
whilst embracing the new doctrine, they might at the same
time work their will with the old Church domains. High
prelates began to reflect whether they might not marry
their cooks, and transmit their electoral dignities, bishop-
rics, and abbacies to their male offspring. The towns'
deputies rejoiced at the prospect of increased independence.
Each had here something to gain, and the secret thoughts
of each were directed to earthly advantages.

But one man was there of whom I am convinced that
he regarded not his own, but the Divine interests which
he represented. This man was Martin Luther, the poor
monk chosen by Providence to shatter the world-empire
of Rome, against which the mightiest emperors and the
boldest sages had already vainly struggled. But Providence well knows upon what shoulders it lays its burdens.
Here, not only spiritual, but also physical power was
necessary. It needed a frame steeled from youth upwards
in monastic chastity and severity to endure the hardships
of such a task. Our dear master was still very thin and
pale, insomuch that the ruddy, well-fed lords of the Diet
looked down almost with compassion on the poor emaciated
man in the monk's black dress. Yet was he quite healthy,
and his nerves were so strong that all the brilliant throng
inspired in him not the slightest fear. His lungs, too,
must have been right lusty, for, after having delivered his
long defence, he was obliged to repeat it in Latin, as the
Emperor did not understand High-German. I become
quite angry every time I think of this; for our dear master
stood beside an open window, exposed to a draught, whilst
the perspiration dropped from his forehead. After such
long speaking, he might well feel much exhausted, and his
lips were no doubt sorely parched. The Duke of Bruns-

wick must have bethought himself that the man would be
very thirsty—at least, we read that he ordered for Martin
Luther from the inn three jugs of the best Eimbeck beer.
I shall never forget this noble deed of the House of
Brunswick.

As of the Reformation, so of its hero, you have in France
quite false ideas.   The immediate cause of this failure to
comprehend the principal actor in that event lies in the
fact that Luther is not only the greatest, but that he is also
the most *German,* man in our history; that in his character are united in their most intensified forms all the
virtues and all the faults of the Germans; that he represents in his own personality the wonderful German land.
He also possessed qualities that we seldom see associated
—nay, that we usually find in the most hostile antagonism.   He was at once a dreamy mystic and a practical
man of action.   His thoughts had not only wings, but also
hands.   He spoke and he acted; he was not only the
tongue, but also the sword of his time.   He was both a
cold, scholastic wordsifter, and an inspired, God-drunk
prophet.   After a long day spent in laboriously working
out dogmatic distinctions, at evening time he would take
his flute and go out to gaze at the stars, and his soul would
dissolve in melody and devotion.   This same man, who
could scold like a fishwife, could also be as gentle as a
sensitive maiden.   He was often as fierce as the storm
that uproots the oak-tree, and then again he was as mild
as the breeze that caresses the violet.   He was full of the
awful reverence of God, full of self-sacrificing devotion to
the Holy Spirit, he could lose himself entirely in pure
spirituality.   And yet he was fully acquainted with the
glories of this earth : he knew how estimable they are; it
was his lips that uttered the famous maxim—

> "Who loves not woman, wine, and song,
> Remains a fool his whole life long."

He was a complete man, I might say, an absolute man, in whom there was no discord between matter and spirit. To call him a spiritualist, therefore, would be as erroneous as to call him a sensualist. How shall I describe him ? He had in him something primordial, incomprehensible, miraculous, such as we find in all providential men ; something naïvely terrible, something boorishly wise, something lofty yet circumscribed, something invincibly dæmoniacal.

Luther's father was a miner at Mannsfeld, and the boy was often with him in his subterranean workplace, in the laboratory of the giant metals, where are the gurgling sources of the great fountains. Perhaps the young heart unconsciously absorbed something of the mysterious forces of Nature, or was bewitched by the pixies. This may have been the cause, too, why so much earthy matter, so much of the dross of passion remained adhering to him, which has so often been made a reproach against him. But the reproach is unjust, for without that earthy admixture he could not have become a man of action. Pure spirit cannot act. Do we not learn from Jung Stilling's "Theory of Ghosts," * that spirits can indeed make themselves visible in distinct form and colour, and can walk, and run, and dance, and otherwise comport themselves like human creatures, but that they are powerless to move any material object, even the smallest table, from its place ?

Praise to Luther ! eternal praise to the dear man whom we have to thank for the deliverance of our most precious possessions, and on whose benefits our life still depends! It little becomes us to complain of the narrowness of his views. The dwarf standing on the shoulders of the giant can indeed see farther than his supporter, especially if he puts on spectacles ; but to such a lofty survey is wanting the elevated feeling, the giant-heart, to which we cannot lay claim. Still less does it become us to pronounce an

* " Theorie der Geisterkunde."—Tr.

austere judgment on his failings; these failings have
profited us more than the virtues of a thousand others.
Neither the subtilty of Erasmus, nor the benignity of
Melancthon, would ever have brought us so far as the
divine brutality of Brother Martin. Yea, these very errors
to which I have already referred have borne the most precious fruits—fruits that are still a solace to all humanity.
From the date of the Diet at which Luther disowned the
authority of the Pope, and publicly declared that "his
doctrine could be refuted only by an appeal to the authority of the Bible itself, or on grounds of reason," a new era
dawned in Germany. The chain by which the holy Boni-
face had bound the German Church to Rome was that day
severed. This Church, which had hitherto formed an
integral portion of the great hierarchy, broke up into religious democracies. Religion itself underwent a change;
the Indo-Gnostic element disappears, and we see the
Judaic - Deistic element again rising into prominence.
Evangelical Christianity emerges. Whenever the most
essential claims of matter are not merely recognised, but
legitimised, religion once more becomes a truth; the priest
becomes a man, and takes a wife and begets children as
God has ordained. On the other hand, God becomes once
more a celestial celibate; the legitimacy of His Son is
disputed; the saints are relieved of their saintship; the
angels have their wings clipped; the Mother of God loses
all claim to the crown of heaven, and is forbidden to work
miracles. In fine, from this time forward, especially since
the natural sciences have made such great progress, miracles cease. Be it that God is chagrined to find natural
philosophers watching His manipulations with such an air
of suspicion, or be it from some other motive; certain it is,
that even in these latter days, wherein religion is in so
great peril, He has disdained to support it by any striking
miracle. Perhaps the new religions that He may hence-

forth establish on earth are to be based solely on reason, which indeed will be much more reasonable. At least in the case of Saint Simonianism, which is the newest religion, no miracle has occurred, with this exception, perhaps, that an old tailor's bill left owing by Saint Simon himself, was paid by his disciples ten years after his death. I still see before me the worthy Père Olinde rising with enthusiasm in the *salle* Taitbout, and exhibiting to the astonished congregation the receipted tailor's bill. Young grocers were amazed at such supernatural testimony; but the tailors began at once to believe!

Yet, if we in Germany, with the loss of miracles through the triumph of Protestantism, also lost much else that was poetic, we have still obtained manifold compensation. Men have become more virtuous, more noble-souled. Protestantism has most favourably influenced that purity of manners and that rigorous performance of duties usually called morality; nay, Protestantism in many communities has taken a direction that identifies it completely with morality. In the lives of the clergy especially do we see a gratifying change. With the abolition of vows of celibacy disappeared likewise the vices and debaucheries of the monks. Amongst the Protestant clergy are often to be found men of such exemplary virtue that even the old Stoics would have had respect for them. One must have travelled on foot as a poor student through North Germany in order to know how much virtue, and, to qualify the word virtue by a really beautiful epithet, how much evangelical virtue is frequently to be found in an unassuming parsonage. How often of a winter evening have I found therein a hospitable welcome—I, a stranger, whose only recommendations were hunger and weariness! When I had well eaten and slept soundly, and was preparing on the morrow morning to set forth again, the old pastor was sure to appear in his dressing-gown to bestow his blessing on my journey—a good act that never brought me misfortune. His kindly and loquacious wife would thrust into my pocket several slices of buttered bread, which proved not less comforting. Behind the mother stood in modest silence the fair daughters of the pastor, with their ruddy cheeks and violet eyes, and the recollection of their timid glances kept my heart warm throughout the whole winter day.

In declaring that his doctrine could be refuted only by an appeal to the Bible or on grounds of reason, Luther conceded to human intelligence the right to explain the Scriptures, and reason was acknowledged as the supreme judge in all religious controversies. Thus was established in Germany spiritual freedom, or, as it is also called, freedom of thought. Thought became a right, and the decisions of reason became legitimate. No doubt for several centuries back men had been permitted to think and to speak with tolerable freedom, and the scholastics had disputed about matters that we can hardly conceive possible to have been mooted in the Middle Ages. But the explanation of this is to be found in the distinction that was made between theological and philosophical truth, a distinction whereby the disputants explicitly guarded themselves against heresy. Besides, such controversies were confined to the lecture-rooms of universities, and were held in a Gothic and abstruse Latin of which the people could not understand a word. The Church had, therefore, little to fear from such discussions. Yet the Church had never expressly sanctioned these proceedings, and so, now and then, by way of protest, she caused a poor scholastic to be burnt. But since Luther's time no such distinction between theological and philosophical truth has been recognised, and men have disputed in the market-place, in the German popular tongue, without reserve or fear. The princes who accepted the Reforma-

tion legitimised this freedom of thought, of which one of
the most important results is German philosophy.

In fact nowhere, not even in Greece, was the human
intellect permitted to develop itself and to express its
thought so freely as in Germany from the middle of last
century till the French Revolution. In Prussia especially an unrestrained liberty of thought prevailed. The
Marquis of Brandenburg perceived that, in becoming
the legitimate king of Prussia by mere strength of the
Protestant principle, he must maintain in its integrity
Protestant freedom of thought. Truly since those days
the state of affairs has changed, and the natural protector
of our Protestant liberty has come to an understanding
with the Ultramontane party to stifle that liberty, and to
this end has traitorously availed himself of a weapon
devised and first directed against us by the Papacy : the
censorship.

Singular ! We Germans are the strongest and most
ingenious of nations. Princes of our race sit on every
European throne ; our Rothschilds govern the exchanges
over the whole earth ; our learned men are sovereigns in
all the sciences ; we have invented gunpowder and the
printing-press ; and yet whoever fires off a pistol in our
country is subjected to a fine of three thalers ; and if any
of us wishes to insert in the *Hamburg Correspondent* these
words : " My dear spouse has given birth to a daughter
beautiful as Freedom !" straightway Dr. Hoffmann * seizes
his red pencil and strikes out " Freedom."

Will this continue much longer ? I know not. But I
know that the question of freedom of the press, at present
so vehemently discussed in Germany, is significantly associated with all the questions of which I have just spoken ;

* The Hamburg censor. As a ing, are not to be found in the early
matter of course, this paragraph, the German editions.—TR.
one preceding it, and the one follow-

and I believe its solution will not be difficult, if we reflect that freedom of the press is nothing else than a consequence of freedom of thought, and therefore a Protestant right. Germany has already given its best blood for rights of this kind, and she may yet again be called upon to enter the lists in defence of the same cause.

This remark is applicable to the question of academical freedom, at present so passionately rousing men's minds in Germany. Since the supposed discovery was made that political agitation, that is to say the love of liberty, is most rampant in the universities, it has on all sides been insinuated to the sovereigns that these institutions ought to be suppressed, or at least converted into ordinary schools of instruction. New schemes have been devised, and the *pro* and *contra* eagerly discussed. But the avowed adversaries of the universities do not seem to have understood any better than such avowed defenders as have hitherto presented themselves, the fundamental principles of the question. They do not comprehend that youth everywhere, and under all forms of discipline, is animated by enthusiasm for liberty ; and that, though the universities were closed, this enthusiasm of the young would assert itself all the more energetically elsewhere, and this, perhaps, in coalition with the youth of the commercial and of the industrial classes. The defenders of the universities content themselves with showing that, with the closing of the universities, German scientific learning also would be swept away ; that it is precisely freedom of academic study that is of value, as affording to the young the best opportunity for varied development : as if a few Greek vocables, or a few rude customs, more or less, had aught to do with the matter ! And what do princes care about science, study, and culture if the sacred security of their thrones is imperilled ! They would be heroic enough to sacrifice all such relative benefits for a single absolute good, for absolute sovereignty. For this possession has been intrusted to them by God, and where Heaven commands, all earthly considerations must give place. There is also misunderstanding of the question on the part of the poor professors, who defend, as well as on the part of the delegates of authority, who attack, the universities. It is only the Catholic propagandists in Germany that rightly comprehend the matter. These pious obscurantists are the most dangerous enemies of our university system, assailing it by lying and fraud; and, when one of them assumes the semblance of taking an affectionate interest in the universities, some jesuitical intrigue is speedily revealed. Well do these cowardly hypocrites know how much is to be won in the game. For with the fall of the universities would fall the Protestant Church, the Church that since the Reformation has been so dependent on the universities that the whole Protestant Church history of these last centuries consists almost exclusively of the records of theological discussions of the learned at Wittenberg, Leipzig, Tübingen, and Halle. The consistories present but a feeble reflection of the theological faculty; with the disappearance of the latter they would lose all support and all character, and sink into a desolate dependence on the ministry, or even on the police.

But let us not indulge too freely in such melancholy reflections, especially as we have still to speak of the providential man by whom so great things were wrought for the German people. I have already shown how through him we attained the widest liberty of thought. For Martin Luther gave us not only freedom of movement, but also the means of movement. To the spirit he gave a body; he gave word to the thought; he created the German language.

This he did by translating the Bible.

The Divine Author of this book seems to have known

as well as we do that the choice of a translator is by no means a matter of indifference. He himself chose His translator, and endowed him with the marvellous faculty of translating out of a dead and already buried language, into a tongue that had not as yet come into existence.

We had, it is true, the Vulgate, which was understood, and the Septuagint, which men were beginning to understand; but the knowledge of Hebrew was quite extinct throughout the Christian world. Only the Jews, who managed to conceal themselves here and there in corners of the earth, still preserved the traditions of this language. Like a ghost that keeps watch over some treasure intrusted to it during its lifetime, so this massacred nation, this ghost-like people cowering in its obscure *ghettos,* kept watch there over the Hebrew Bible. Into these evil-reputed hiding-places German men of learning might be seen secretly stealing down in order to discover the treasure, to acquire a knowledge of Hebrew. As soon as the Catholic priesthood perceived the danger that thus threatened them, that the people might by such a side-way attain an acquaintance with the true Word of God, and thereby discover the Romish falsifications, they would fain have suppressed Jewish tradition, and they set to work to destroy all Hebrew books. Thus began on the banks of the Rhine that book-persecution, against which our admirable Doctor Reuchlin so gloriously fought. The theologians of Cologne, who were active in the matter, particularly Hochstraaten, were by no means so devoid of intelligence as Ulrich von Hutten, Reuchlin's valiant champion, represents them in his *Litteræ Obscurorum Virorum.* They attempted nothing less than the suppression of the Hebrew language. When Reuchlin was victorious, Luther was able to begin his work. From a letter written by him at this time to Reuchlin, Luther seems already to have felt how important was the victory

that had been gained,—gained too by one in a dependent
and difficult position,—whereas he, the Augustin monk,
was perfectly independent. Very naïvely does Luther say
in this letter : " *Ego nihil timeo, quia nihil habeo.*"

But how Luther succeeded in creating the language
into which he translated the Bible, remains a mystery to
me even to this hour. The old Suabian dialect had totally
disappeared, along with the chivalrous poetry of the
Hohenstaufen imperial era. The old Saxon dialect, so-
called low-German, was in use throughout only a portion of Northern Germany, and despite all efforts that
have been made it has never been found possible to adapt
it to literary purposes. Had Luther employed for his
translation of the Bible the language that is spoken to-day
in Saxony, Adelung would have been right in maintaining
that Saxon, especially the dialect of Meissen, was the
true high-German, that is to say, our literary language.
But this error was long ago refuted, though I must here
draw special attention to it on account of its being still
quite current in France. Modern Saxon never was a
dialect of the Germans,—as little was it so as Silesian ; the
former like the latter, having a strong Slavonian admixture. I therefore frankly confess that I know not what
was the origin of the language we find in Luther's Bible.
But this I know that, through his Bible which the new-
born press, the black art, scattered by thousands of copies
amongst the people, the Lutheran language spread in a
few years over the whole of Germany, and was raised to
the rank of a written tongue. This written tongue holds
its place to this day in Germany, and gives to that politically and religiously dismembered nation a literary unity.
Such an inestimable gain may well make amends to us
for any loss in the later development of the language of
that internal expressiveness we are accustomed to find in
languages having their origin in a single dialect. There

is no want, however, of such expressiveness in the language of Luther's Bible, and this old book is a perennial source of rejuvenescence for our tongue. Every expression and every idiom to be found in Luther's Bible is essentially German; an author may unhesitatingly employ it; and as this book is in the hands of the poorest classes, they have no need of any special learned instruction to enable them to express themselves in a literary style. This circumstance will, when the political revolution takes place in Germany, result in strange phenomena. Liberty will everywhere be able to speak, and its speech will be Biblical.

Luther's original writings have also contributed to fix the German language. Owing to their polemical passionateness, they pierced deeply into the heart of his time. Their tone is not always delicate; but not even a religious revolution can be made with orange blossom. Oftentimes the stubborn tree root can be cleft only by the stubborn wedge. In the Bible Luther's speech is always restrained within the bounds of a certain dignity by reverence for the ever-present Spirit of God. In his controversial writings, on the contrary, he abandons himself to a plebeian vulgarity that is often as repulsive as it is grandiose. His expressions and his metaphors resemble the colossal stone images to be seen in Hindoo or Egyptian temple grottos; their gaudy colouring and fantastic hideousness both repel and fascinate us. By reason of this uncouth granite style the daring monk often appears like a religious Danton, a preacher of the Mountain, who from his lofty elevation hurls down his strange word-blocks on the heads of his adversaries.

But more remarkable and more significant than these prose works are Luther's poems, the hymns that budded forth in his soul amidst the conflicts and troubles of his days. Oftentimes they resemble a flower blooming on a bare rock; oftentimes they are like a moonbeam shimmering across a tossing sea. Luther loved music; he even wrote a treatise on the art; and his songs are extremely melodious. In this respect also he merits the name of the Swan of Eisleben. He was, however, anything but a mild swan in many of the songs in which he rouses the courage of his followers and inspires himself with fiercest ardour for the combat. A true war-song was that defiant lay with which he and his companions entered Worms. The old cathedral trembled at such unwonted strains, and the ravens were terrified in their obscure nests up in the church towers. This song—the Marseillaise Hymn of the Reformation—preserves even yet its power of inspiring men, and perhaps we may ere long have need in similar combats of the old mail-clad words :—

> A strong tower is the Lord our God,
> A trusty shield and weapon ;
> He frees us in our mighty need
> From all the ills that happen.
> The old and wicked fiend
> Now earnestly has meaned ;
> Great power, much deceit,
> His dreadful armour meet ;
> On earth is not his fellow.
>
> For our own power could not avail,
> We soon should find an ending ;
> Yet bravely for us will prevail
> The man of God's own sending.
> Seek'st, who this may be ?
> Jesus Christ, 'tis He,
> The Lord Sabaoth,
> And sure no other God
> For us the field maintaineth.
>
> And though the devils filled all lands,
> Seeking our soul's devouring ;
> We need not greatly fear their bands,
> Our help is overpowering.

> The prince of this earth,
> Though full of grim wrath,
> Must yet fail of his plan ;
> He lieth under a ban,
> A mere word can o'erthrow him.
>
> This word they may not take away,
> Nor yet have thanks for leaving ;
> God's on our side with grace and power,
> To Him our souls are cleaving.
> Take, if ye choose, our life,
> Goods, honour, child, and wife,
> Let go as they may ;
> Your gain's but small, we say,—
> The Kingdom ours remaineth.[5]

I have shown how we have to thank our dear Doctor Martin Luther for the intellectual freedom that was needed for the development of modern literature. I have shown how he also created for us the word, the speech wherein this new literature might express itself. I have still to add that he was himself the precursor of this literature; that our polite literature properly so-called begins with Luther; that his spiritual songs prove themselves to be its first important monument and already reveal its distinctive character. Whoever would speak of modern German literature must therefore begin with Luther, and not with that narrow-souled citizen of Nüremberg called Hans Sachs, as has been done through the bad faith of certain writers of the Romantic school. Hans Sachs, the troubadour of the honourable guild of shoemakers, whose master-song is but a crude parody of the ancient lays of minstrelsy, and his dramas mere clumsy travesties of the old mysteries;—this pedantic buffoon, with his painful aping of the free simplicity of the Middle Ages, may perhaps be regarded as the last poet of the olden time, but can in no sense be considered the earliest poet of the new age.[6]

PART SECOND.

In the first part of this book we have treated of the great religious revolution represented in Germany by Martin Luther. We have now to speak of the philosophic revolution which, as the offspring of the religious revolution, is nothing else than the last consequence of Protestantism.

But before proceeding to relate how this revolution found its outburst through Immanuel Kant, it is necessary to refer to the philosophical events that preceded it abroad, to the significance of Spinoza, to the fate of the philosophy of Leibnitz, to the mutual relations between this philosophy and religion, and to their discords. We shall, however, keep constantly in view those questions of philosophy to which we attach a social significance, and towards whose solution the social co-operates with the religious element.

We have here to deal with the question of the nature of God. God is the beginning and the end of all wisdom, say believers in their humility, and the philosopher in all the pride of his knowledge is compelled to assent to this pious axiom.

Not Bacon, as we are accustomed to be taught, but René Descartes is the father of modern philosophy, and we shall proceed to demonstrate very clearly the degree of affinity between him and German philosophy.

René Descartes is a Frenchman, and to great France belongs the fame of the initiative. But great France, the noisy, stirring, talkative land of the French, has never been a fitting abode for philosophy, which perhaps will never flourish on French soil.   So assuredly felt René Descartes, who betook himself to Holland, to the peaceful, silent land of track-boats and Dutchmen.   Here he wrote his philosophical works.   Only in that country was it possible for him to free his intellect from traditional formalism, and to construct a complete system of philosophy out of pure thought, indebted neither to faith nor to empiricism—a condition ever since demanded of all true philosophy. Only in such a country could he plunge deeply enough into the intellectual abyss to be able to surprise thought in the ultimate grounds of self-consciousness, and thus establish self-consciousness through the process of thought in the world-famed axiom, *Cogito, ergo sum.*

But perhaps nowhere else than in Holland could Descartes have ventured to teach a philosophy that conflicted openly with every tradition of the past.   To him is due the honour of having established the autonomy of philosophy : philosophy no longer needed to solicit from theology permission to think for itself ; it could now take its place alongside the latter as an independent science.   I do not say in opposition to the latter ; for, in Descartes' time, it was an acknowledged principle that the truths at which we arrive through philosophy are ultimately identical with those transmitted by religion.   The scholastics, as I have already remarked, had, on the contrary, not only conceded to religion the supremacy over philosophy, but had also declared the latter, from the moment it came into conflict with the dogmas of religion, to be mere futile pastime, mere wordy contention.   The prime object of the scholastics was to express their thoughts, no matter under what conditions.   They said, " Once one is one ; " but they added with a smile, "yet this is only another error of human reason, which is always at fault when it leads to contradiction of the decisions of the Œcumenical Councils;

'Once one is three,' and that is the absolute truth, long since revealed to us in the name of the Father, of the Son, and of the Holy Ghost!" The scholastics secretly formed a philosophic opposition to the Church ; publicly, however, they feigned the meekest submissiveness ; in many instances they even fought the battles of the Church, and paraded as attendants at its processions, somewhat as the French deputies of the opposition did at the ceremonies of the Restoration.

The comedy of the scholastics lasted more than six centuries, and it became more and more trivial. In destroying scholasticism Descartes likewise destroyed the effete opposition of the Middle Ages ; the old brooms were worn out with long usage, they were too thickly covered with offscourings, and the new age had need of new brooms. After every revolution the former opposition must abdicate, otherwise great follies will be perpetrated. We have had experience of such things. In the times of which I speak, it was not so much the Catholic Church herself as her old adversaries, the rearguard of scholasticism, that took up arms against the Cartesian philosophy. For not till 1663 did the Pope anathematise this philosophy.

I may presuppose that Frenchmen are sufficiently acquainted with the philosophy of their great countryman, and it is here unnecessary for me to show how two doctrines, the most directly opposed, have both derived from that philosophy the necessary framework of their systems. I refer to the doctrines of Idealism and Materialism.

As these two doctrines have usually been designated, especially in France, Spiritualism and Sensualism, and as I am accustomed to employ these latter terms in a different acceptation, it is necessary, in order to prevent confusion of ideas, that I should more clearly define these expressions.

Since the earliest times two opposite views have existed

regarding the nature of human thought, that is to say, concerning the ultimate sources of intellectual cognition, concerning the origin of ideas. Some hold that we receive ideas only from without, that the mind is merely an empty alembic wherein the impressions gathered in by the senses are elaborated, much as the food we partake of is assimilated in the stomach. To employ a better metaphor, this class of thinkers considers the mind as a *tabula rasa*, whereon experience is daily writing something new in accordance with certain determined rules of caligraphy. Others, holding the opposite view, assert that ideas are born with man, that the human mind is the primary seat of ideas, and that the external world, experience, and the intermediary senses only bring us to the knowledge of what was already present in the mind, only awaken there the dormant ideas.

The former view has received the name of sensualism, sometimes that of empiricism; the latter has been called spiritualism, sometimes also rationalism. But misconceptions may easily result from this nomenclature. For these two names, spiritualism and sensualism, have for some time been employed to designate two social systems that assert themselves in every manifestation of existence. We assign, then, the name spiritualism to that outrageous assumption of the human spirit, which, striving after exclusive glorification of itself, endeavours to trample under foot, or at least to stultify, matter. We bestow the name sensualism on that opposition, which, revolting against this pretension, has for its aim the rehabilitation of matter and the vindication of the inalienable rights of the senses, without thereby denying to the spirit its rights or even its supremacy.

These two systems have stood opposed as far back as human memory can reach. For in all ages are to be found men in whom the capacity for enjoyment is incomplete,

men with stunted senses and compunctious frames, for
whom all the grapes in this garden of God are sour, who
see in every paradise-apple the enticing serpent, who seek
in abnegation their triumph, and in suffering their sole joy.
On the other hand, we find in all ages men of robust
growth, natures filled with the pride of life, who fain carry
their heads right haughtily; all the stars and the roses
greet them with sympathetic smile; they listen delightedly
to the melodies of the nightingale and of Rossini; they are
enamoured of good fortune and of the flesh of Titian's
pictures; and to their hypocritical companions for whom
such things are a torment, they answer, in the words of
Shakespeare's character, " Dost thou think because thou
art virtuous, there shall be no more cakes and ale ? " *

I leave, then, to these two social systems the names
Spiritualism and Sensualism. But when speaking of the
philosophical opinions regarding the origin of our knowledge I prefer the terms Idealism and Materialism, desig-
nating by the former the doctrine of innate ideas, of ideas
a priori, and by the latter the doctrine of cognition through
experience, through the senses, the doctrine of ideas *a
posteriori*.

It is a very significant fact that the idealistic side of the
Cartesian philosophy has never been successfully followed
up in France. Some celebrated Jansenists pursued for a
time this direction; but they quickly lost themselves in
Christian spiritualism. It may have been this circumstance that brought discredit on idealism amongst the
French. Nations have an instinctive presentiment of
what they require in order to fulfil their mission. The

* This characteristic paragraph
does not appear in any but the most
recent German editions of Heine's
works. Heine had himself deleted
it in the original manuscript recovered by Dr. Strodtmann, who
suggests as the cause of its omission
that the quotation with which it concludes is employed in a different application further on.—Tr.

French were already on the march towards that political revolution which did not break out till the close of the eighteenth century, and for which they had need of a headsman's axe and of a materialistic philosophy equally cold and keen.   Christian spiritualism was a combatant in the ranks of their enemies ; sensualism therefore became their natural ally.   French sensualists being ordinarily materialists, the erroneous notion came to obtain that sensualism was but a product of materialism. No ; sensualism may with equal right claim to be the result of pantheism, and as such it appears beautiful and imposing. Yet we would not seek in the least to detract from the services rendered by French materialism. It was an efficacious antidote against the evil of the past, a desperate remedy for a desperate disease, a sovereign panacea for an infected people. French philosophers chose John Locke as their master ; he was the saviour of whom they had need. His " Essay on the Human Understanding " became their gospel ; they were ready to swear by it. John Locke had gone to the school of Descartes, and from him had learned all that an Englishman can learn—mechanics, analytical method, and the art of reckoning. There was but one thing that he could not understand ; namely, innate ideas. He therefore brought to perfection the doctrine according to which all our knowledge is derived from without by means of experience. He reduced the human mind to a species of calculating machine ; in his hands the whole man became a piece of English mechanism. This also applies to man as constructed by the disciples of Locke, though they sought to distinguish themselves from their master under various denominations. They had a perfect dread of the ultimate results of their leading principle, and the disciple of Condillac was horror-stricken at being classed in the same category with Helvetius, even with Holbach, or possibly with Lamétrie. Yet such a classification was inevitable, and I may therefore give to one and all of the French philosophers of the eighteenth century, and to their successors in our time, the name of materialists. *L'homme machine* is the most consistent result of French philosophy, and the title of this book betrays it at once as the last word of this conception of the universe.

Most of these materialists were also partisans of deism; for a machine presupposes a mechanician, and the highest perfection of such a machine consists in its capacity for recognising and appreciating the technical skill of such an artificer, as displayed either in its own construction or in his other works.

Materialism has fulfilled its mission in France. It is perhaps at the present moment busy accomplishing the same task in England; and it is on the system of Locke that the revolutionary sects in that country, especially the Benthamites, the apostles of utility, take their stand. These latter are men of powerful intellect; they have possessed themselves of the right lever with which John Bull may be set in motion. John Bull is a born materialist, and his Christian spiritualism is for the most part traditional hypocrisy, or even mere material dulness; his flesh resigns itself because the spirit does not come to its aid. In Germany it is quite otherwise, and German revolutionists deceive themselves in supposing that a materialistic philosophy is favourable to their projects.

Germany has always manifested a repugnance towards materialism; hence she remained during a century and a half the true home of idealism. The Germans also went to the school of Descartes, whose great disciple is called Gottfried Wilhelm Leibnitz. As Locke pursued the materialistic tendency of his master, so Leibnitz followed the idealistic tendency. In Leibnitz we find the doctrine of innate ideas in its most decisive form. In his "New Essays on the Human Understanding" he combated the principles of Locke. With Leibnitz there sprang up amongst Germans a great ardour for philosophical studies. He awakened the minds of men, and led them into new paths. On account of the natural suavity, the religious sentiment that animated his writings, his opponents became partially reconciled to the boldness of his views, and the effect was prodigious. The hardihood of this thinker exhibited itself especially in his theory of Monads, one of the most remarkable hypotheses that have ever proceeded from the brain of a philosopher. It is also the best service he has rendered, for it embodies a presentiment of the most important laws that have been accepted by modern philosophy. The theory of monads was but a crude method of formulating those laws that are now proclaimed in better formulas by natural philosophers. But here, instead of the word " law," I ought, properly speaking, to employ the word " formula ; " for Newton observes with great truth that what we call law in nature has no real existence, and that it is merely formulas that come to the aid of intelligence as explaining a succession of phenomena in nature. Of all the works of Leibnitz, the " Theodicee " is the one most spoken of in Germany. Yet it is his feeblest production. This book, like several other writings in which Leibnitz expresses his religious sentiments, has obtained for its author an evil reputation, and has caused him to be cruelly misunderstood. His enemies have accused him of maudlin sentimentality and weakness of intellect; his friends, in defending, have proved him an accomplished hypocrite. The character of Leibnitz was for long a subject of controversy amongst us : the most partial critics could not absolve him from the accusation of duplicity ; his most eager detractors were the freethinkers and the men of enlightenment. How could they pardon in a philosopher defence of the Trinity, eternal punishment, and the divinity of Christ ! Their tolerance did not extend so far as that. But Leibnitz was neither fool nor knave, and by the lofty harmony of his intellect he was well able to defend Christianity in its integrity. I say, in its integrity, for he defended it against semi-Christianity. He established the consistency of the orthodox as opposed to the inconsistency of their adversaries. More than this he never attempted. He thus stood at that point of indifference where diverse systems appear as merely different sides of the same truth. Schelling afterwards acknowledged this standpoint, and Hegel has scientifically established it as a system of systems. In a similar manner Leibnitz engaged in an attempt at a harmony between Plato and Aristotle. In these latter days the attempt has been often enough renewed. Is the problem solved?

No, assuredly not! for this problem is nothing less than an adjustment of the quarrel between idealism and materialism. Plato is a thorough idealist and knows only inborn, or rather *with*-born ideas; man brings his ideas with him into the world, and when he becomes conscious of them, they appear to him as recollections of a former state of existence. Hence the vagueness and mysticism of Plato: he merely recollects more or less clearly. With Aristotle, on the contrary, everything is clear, intelligible, certain; for his cognitions are not reminiscences of a premundane state; he receives everything from experience, and knows how to classify everything in the most precise manner. He stands out therefore as the model for all empiricists; and the latter cannot sufficiently thank God that He made him the teacher of Alexander, whose conquests afforded him so many opportunities for the advancement of science; and that his victorious scholar should have presented him with so many thousand talents of gold for zoological researches. The old master employed the money very conscientiously, and was thereby enabled to dissect numerous specimens of mammals, and to obtain a great collection of stuffed birds; all which afforded him scope for the most important observations. But the great biped which he had right before his eyes, which he had himself reared, and which was far more remarkable than all the rest of the world-menagerie, he unfortunately overlooked and omitted to investigate. In fact, he has left us totally without information regarding the nature of that youthful king, the wonder and enigma of whose life and deeds still awaken our amazement. What was Alexander? What sought he? Was he a madman or a god? To this day we cannot tell. But Aristotle's information is all the more complete concerning Assyrian quadrupeds, Indian parrots, and Greek tragedies, which latter he also dissected.

Plato and Aristotle! They are not merely the representatives of two systems, they are the types of two different species of humanity, which since time immemorial, under every variety of garb, have stood opposed to each other in more or less hostile attitude. Especially throughout the Middle Ages, and down to our own time, has the conflict been maintained; and the progress of this conflict forms the essential part of Christian Church history. The talk is always of Plato and Aristotle, though disguised under other names. Dreamy, mystical, Platonic natures find revealed in the depths of their being the Christian idea and its corresponding symbols. Practical, methodical, Aristotelian natures construct out of this idea and its symbols a definite system, a dogma, and a worship. The Church in the end embraces within its pale both classes —the one taking its position as a secular clergy, the other intrenching itself in a monastic life, yet each continuing to wage incessant warfare upon the other. In the Protestant Church the same conflict exhibits itself in the schism between pietists and the followers of orthodoxy, who correspond in a certain degree to the mystics and the dogmatists of Catholicism. The Protestant pietists are mystics without imagination, and the Protestant orthodox are dogmatists without intelligence.

We find these two Protestant parties engaged in desperate conflict in the time of Leibnitz, whose philosophy afterwards intervened when Christian Wolf, having made himself master of it, adapted it to the necessities of the time, and, what was of the utmost importance, lectured on it in the German language. But before speaking of this pupil of Leibnitz, of the results of his labours, and of the later destiny of Lutheranism, we must make mention of the providential man who, simultaneously with Locke and Leibnitz, formed himself in the school of Descartes, who was for long regarded with derision and hatred, but who in our day has been raised to the throne of intellectual supremacy.

I speak of Benedict Spinoza.

One great genius forms itself from another less by assimilation than by friction. One diamond polishes another. Thus the philosophy of Descartes in no sense originated, it merely advanced that of Spinoza. Hence we find in the disciple the method of the master; this is a great gain. We also find in Spinoza, as in Descartes, a mode of demonstration borrowed from mathematics; this is a grievous fault. The mathematical form gives to Spinoza's writings a harsh exterior. But this is like the hard shell of the almond; the kernel is all the more agreeable. In reading Spinoza's works we become conscious of a feeling such as pervades us at the sight of great Nature in her most life-like state of repose; we behold a forest of heaven-reaching thoughts whose blossoming topmost boughs are tossing like waves of the sea, whilst their immovable stems are rooted in the eternal earth. There is a peculiar, indescribable fragrance about the writings of Spinoza. We seem to breathe in them the air of the future.

Perhaps the spirit of the Hebrew prophets still hovered over their late-born descendant.   There is, withal, an earnestness in him, a self-conscious bearing, a solemn grandeur of thought that certainly seems as though it were inherited; for Spinoza belonged to one of those martyr-families driven into exile by the most Catholic kings of Spain.   Added to this was the patience of the Dutchman, which never belies itself either in the life or in the writings of the man.

It is beyond a doubt that the whole course of Spinoza's life was free from blame, and pure and spotless as the life of his divine cousin, Jesus Christ.   Like him, too, he suffered for his doctrine; like him he wore the crown of thorns.   Wherever a great spirit utters its thought, *there* is Golgotha.

Dear reader, if ever thou shouldst visit Amsterdam, bid some cicerone show thee the Spanish synagogue.   It is a beautiful building, having its roof resting on four colossal pillars.   In the midst stands the pulpit from which was pronounced the curse on the despiser of the Mosaic law, the Hidalgo don Benedict de Spinoza.   On such an occasion, a buck's-horn, called the *Shofar,* was blown.   There must be something quite terrible about this horn; for, as I once read in the life of Solomon Maimon, as the Rabbi of Altona was endeavouring to lead him, the pupil of Kant, back to the old faith, and as he stubbornly persisted in his philosophical heresies, the Rabbi resorted to threats and, holding up the Shofar, inquired in tones of awe, "Know'st thou what this is?"   But when the pupil of Kant replied with calm indifference, "It is the horn of a buck," the horror-stricken Rabbi fell backwards on the ground.

At the excommunication of Spinoza there was a solemn accompaniment on this horn; he was ceremoniously expelled the communion of Israel, and declared unworthy henceforth to bear the name of Jew.   His Christian enemies were magnanimous enough to leave him the name. But the Jews, the Swiss-guard of Deism, were inexorable, and the spot is still pointed out in front of the Spanish synagogue at Amsterdam where they attempted to stab Spinoza with their long daggers.

I could not refrain from drawing special attention to these personal misfortunes of the man. He was trained not merely in the lessons of the school, but also in those of life. Herein is he distinguished from most philosophers, and in his writings we recognise the indirect influence of his life-training. Theology was for him something more than a mere science. So also was politics; for with this too he made practical acquaintance. The father of his be- trothed was hung for political offences in the Netherlands; and nowhere else in the world are people so badly hung as in the Netherlands. You have no idea with what pre- parations and ceremonies the operation is accompanied. The delinquent is already dead with *ennui*, and the spectator has abundant leisure for reflection. I am per- suaded, then, that Benedict Spinoza reflected very deeply on the execution of the old Van Ende, and as previously he had comprehended religion with its daggers, so now he comprehended politics with the cord. Evidence of this is to be found in his "Tractatus Politicus."

My task consists merely in pointing out how these phi- losophers come to be more or less nearly related, and I confine myself to indicating their degrees of relationship and their genealogy. The philosophy of Spinoza, third son of René Descartes, as he enunciates it in his principal work, the "Ethics," is as widely different from the mate- rialism of his brother Locke as from the idealism of his brother Leibnitz. Spinoza does not torment himself with analytical inquiry into the ultimate grounds of our cogni- tions. He gives us his grand synthesis, his explanation of Deity.

Benedict Spinoza teaches: there is but one substance, which is God. This one substance is infinite; it is absolute: all finite substances emanate from it, are contained in it, emerge out of it, are submerged in it; they have only a relative, transient, accidental existence. The absolute substance reveals itself to us as clearly in the form of infinite thought as in the form of infinite extension. These two, infinite thought and infinite extension, are the two attributes of the absolute substance. We recognise only these two attributes; but God, the absolute substance, has perhaps many other attributes that we do not know. " *Non dico, me Deum omnino cognoscere, sed me quædam ejus attributa, non autem omnia, neque maximam intelligere partem.*"

Nothing but sheer unreason and malice could bestow on such a doctrine the qualification of " atheism." No one has ever spoken more sublimely of Deity than Spinoza. Instead of saying that he denied God, one might say that he denied man. All finite things are to him but modes of the infinite substance; all finite substances are contained in God; the human mind is but a luminous ray of infinite thought; the human body but an atom of infinite extension: God is the infinite cause of both, of mind and of body, *natura naturans.*

In a letter to Madame du Deffant, Voltaire professes himself quite charmed at a sally of this lady's, who had said that everything that man cannot know is assuredly of such a nature that it would profit him nothing to know. I might apply this remark to the passage from Spinoza just quoted in his own words, according to which, besides the two knowable attributes of thought and extension, there may pertain to Deity other attributes that cannot be known. What we cannot know has no value for us, at least no value from a social point of view, where it is a question of realising in sensible fact what the intellect perceives. In our explanation of the being of God, we have therefore regard only to these two knowable attributes. And, besides, everything that we call attribute of Deity is, after all, but a different form of our intuition, and these different forms are identical in the absolute substance. Thought is, after all, but invisible extension, and extension is but visible thought. Here we come into contact with the leading axiom of the German Philosophy of Identity, which in reality does not differ from the doctrine of Spinoza. Let Schelling protest as eagerly as he may that his philosophy is something else than Spinozism, that it is rather "a living amalgam of the ideal and the real," that it is distinguishable from Spinozism "as the perfection of Greek statuary is distinguishable from the rigid Egyptian originals;" I must none the less emphatically declare that in his first period, at the time when he was still a philosopher, Schelling is not to be distinguished in the slightest degree from Spinoza. He has only taken a different road to arrive at the same philosophy. I have yet to elucidate this when I come to explain how Kant opened up a new path, how Fichte followed him, how Schelling, in pursuing still further the footsteps of Fichte, having gone astray in the gloomy forest of the Philosophy of Nature, at last found himself face to face with the great figure of Benedict Spinoza.

The only merit of the modern Philosophy of Nature lies in demonstrating, in the clearest manner, the eternal parallelism that exists between spirit and matter. I say spirit and matter, and I employ these expressions as equivalents for what Spinoza calls thought and extension; I also regard these expressions as synonymous with what our German philosophers call spirit and nature, or the ideal and the real.

In what follows I shall designate by the word Pantheism, not so much the system as the point of view of

Spinoza. Pantheism, like Deism, assumes the unity of God ; but the God of the pantheists is in the world itself, not by informing it with his divinity, as St. Augustin endeavoured to explain by comparing God to a great lake and the world to a sponge floating in the middle of it and absorbing Deity: no, the world is not merely God-distended, God-impregnated, it is identical with God. God, called by Spinoza the Sole Substance, and by German philosophers the Absolute, " is All that is;" He is matter as well as spirit, both are equally divine, and he that insults the sanctity of matter is as impious as he that sins against the Holy Ghost.

The God of the pantheists, then, is distinguished from the God of the deists by being in the world itself, whereas the latter is outside of, or, what is the same thing, is above the world. The God of deism governs the world from above as an establishment apart from him. It is only with regard to the mode of this government that deists differ among themselves. The Hebrews conceive God as a tyrant armed with thunder ; Christians, as a loving father; the disciples of Rousseau and the whole Genevese school. regard him as a skilful artist, who has fashioned the world somewhat as their fathers constructed watches, and as experienced critics they admire the work and praise the celestial workman.

In the eyes of the deist, who assumes an extra-mundane or supra-mundane God, the spirit alone is holy, because he regards it as the divine breath which the Creator of the universe has breathed into the human body, the work of his hands formed of the dust of the earth. Hence the Jews looked on the body as a despicable thing, as the pitiful envelope of the *Rouach hakodasch*, of the divine breath, of the spirit; and to the latter only would they accord consideration, reverence, and worship. The Jews are therefore in quite a special sense the people of the spirit, chaste, temperate, serious, abstract, stiff-necked, fit to be martyrs; and their sublimest flower is Jesus Christ. He is, in the true sense of the word, the incarnate spirit; and full of deepest significance is the beautiful legend that he is the offspring of a pure virgin conceived by the sole operation of the Spirit.

But if the Jews regarded the body merely with contempt, Christians, the *Ultras* of spiritualism, have gone much farther on the same road, and look upon the body as something to be reprobated, as wicked, as the evil thing itself. Thus, several centuries after the birth of Christ we see a religion arise that will form an eternal subject of astonishment to the historian, and that will compel the shuddering amazement of latest generations. Yes, Christianity is a grand, a holy religion, full of infinite blessedness, a religion that seeks to conquer for the spirit the most absolute domination on earth. But such a religion was far too sublime, far too pure, far too good for this world, where its idea could only be proclaimed in theory, but could never be realised in practice. The attempt to realise it has produced in human history an infinite number of heroic deeds, which will afford to poets of all ages ample themes for story and song. But the endeavour to realise the Christian idea has, as we at last come to see, most lamentably failed, and the abortive attempt has cost humanity incalculable sacrifices; sacrifices whose calamitous effects are visible in the social distemper that afflicts all Europe at the present day. If, as many believe, humanity is still in its adolescence, then Christianity is doubtless one of the most generous illusions of youth, though it does far more honour to the heart than to the head. Christianity having abandoned to Cæsar and to his Jewish chamberlains matter and all temporal things, contented itself with denying the supremacy of the former, and with stigmatising the latter in public opinion. But lo! the detested sword and the despised riches obtain in the end supreme power, and the representatives of spiritualism are obliged to come to an understanding with them. Yes, and this understanding has even become a mutual alliance. Not the priests of Rome only, but those also of England and of Prussia, in short, all privileged priesthoods have associated themselves with Cæsar and his confederates for the oppression of the peoples. The result of this alliance is but to hasten the overthrow of the religion of spiritualism. A portion of the priesthood already comprehends this, and in order to save religion they assume the pretence of renouncing the pernicious alliance and seek to range themselves in our ranks by adopting our colours.

Vain efforts, futile endeavours! Humanity yearns after more solid food than the symbolic blood and flesh of the Eucharist. Humanity smiles compassionately at the ideals of its youth, that have failed in realisation in spite of all its painful attempts; and it grows manfully practical. Humanity in our day worships a system of earthly utility; it has serious thoughts about establishing itself in citizen prosperity, about a reasonably ordered household, about securing comfort for its old age. The thing of prime importance at the moment is its restoration to health, for we still feel a great weakness in all our members; the holy vampires of the Middle Ages have sucked out of us so much life-blood! And after this it will still be necessary to offer grand expiatory sacrifices to matter, in order to atone for old offences against it. It might even be expedient to institute holy-day revels, and to indemnify matter for its past sufferings; for Christianity, unable to annihilate, has on all occasions sought to bring disgrace upon matter: it has depreciated the noblest delights, the senses have been forced to become hypocritical, and everywhere there has been deceit and sin. We must reclothe women in new chemises and in new sentiments, and all our emotions must be passed through a process of disinfection as after having undergone the ravages of a plague.

Thus the immediate aim of all our modern institutions is the rehabilitation of matter, its restoration to former dignity, its moral recognition, its religious sanctification, its reconciliation with the spirit; Purusa is re-wedded to Pakriti; from their violent separation, as the Indian myth so ingeniously symbolises, the great laceration of the world, Evil, has arisen.

Can you tell us, then, what the evil of the world signifies? The spiritualists have always made it a reproach against us that, in the pantheistic view, the distinction between good and evil is lost. But evil is in part merely an erroneous conception of the world by the spiritualists; and in part it is an actual product of their arrangement of mundane affairs. According to their view, matter is in itself an evil thing; which is surely nothing less than a calumny and fearful blasphemy against God. Matter becomes evil only when it is forced into secret conspiracy against the usurpation of the spirit, when it is stigmatised by the spirit and then degrades itself through loss of self-respect, or when with the hatred of despair it avenges itself on the spirit; and thus evil is a result of the arrangement of the world by the spiritualists.

God is identical with the world: he manifests himself in plants, which unconsciously live a cosmic-magnetic life; he manifests himself in animals which, in the dream of their sensuous life, experience an existence more or less torpid. But he manifests himself most gloriously in man, who feels and thinks at the same time, who is capable of distinguishing his own individuality from objective nature, whose intellect already bears within itself the ideas that present themselves to him in the phenomenal world. In man Deity reaches self-consciousness, and this self-consciousness Deity again reveals through man. But this revelation does not take place in and through individual man, but in and through collective humanity; and this in such wise that each man comprehends and represents but a portion of the God-universe; whereas collective humanity comprehends and represents in idea and in reality the whole God-universe. Every nation is perhaps endowed with the mission of recognising and manifesting a portion of this God-universe, of comprehending a series of facts and of realising a series of ideas, and of transmitting the result to succeeding races on whom a like mission is imposed. God is therefore the real hero of universal history : history is but his eternal thought, his eternal action, his word, his deed; and of entire humanity we may justly say it is an incarnation of God.

It is an error to suppose that this religion, Pantheism, leads men to indifference. On the contrary, the consciousness of his divinity will inspire man with enthusiasm for its manifestation, and from this moment will the really noble achievements of true heroism glorify the earth.

The political revolution, based on the principles of French materialism, will find in the pantheists not opponents but allies; allies, however, who have drawn their convictions from a deeper source—from a religious synthesis. We promote the welfare of matter, the material happiness of nations, not, like the materialists, from a contempt for the spirit, but because we know that the divinity of man reveals itself also in his corporeal form, that misery destroys or debases the body, God's image, and that thereby the spirit likewise is involved in ruin. The great word of the revolution pronounced by St. Just, " Bread is the right of the people," is translated by us, " Bread is the divine right of man." We are fighting not for the human rights of the people, but for the divine rights of humanity. In this and in much else we differ from the men of the revo-

lution. We do not wish to be sans-culottists, nor frugal
citizens, nor unassuming presidents; we are for founding a
democracy of terrestrial gods, equal in glory, in blessedness, and in sanctity. You demand simple modes of dress,
austere morals, and unspiced pleasures; we, on the contrary, desire nectar and ambrosia, purple mantles, costly perfumes, luxury and splendour, dances of laughing nymphs,
music and comedies. Be not therefore angry with us,
virtuous republicans! To your censorious reproaches
we reply in the words of Shakespeare's character:—
"Dost thou think because thou art virtuous, there shall
be no more cakes and ale?"

The Saint Simonians comprehended and desired something analogous; but the soil was unfavourable, and they
were repressed, for the time at least, by the surrounding
materialism. They have been better appreciated in Germany, for Germany is now the fertile soil of pantheism.
This is the religion of our greatest thinkers, of our best
artists, and in Germany deism, as I shall presently explain,
was long ago theoretically destroyed. No one says it, but
every one knows it: pantheism is the open secret of Germany. We have, in fact, outgrown deism. We are free,
and we want no thundering tyrants; we have reached
majority and can dispense with paternal care. Neither
are we the work of a great mechanician. Deism is a
religion for slaves, for children, for Genevese, for watch-
makers.

Pantheism is the occult religion of Germany, and this
result was foreseen by those German writers who, fifty
years ago, let loose their zealotry against Spinoza. The
most furious of these adversaries of Spinoza was F. H.
Jacobi, who is occasionally honoured by being ranked
among German philosophers. He was but a gossiping old
woman, disguised in the mantle of philosophy, who, having
insinuated himself amongst philosophers, began by whin-

ing to them about his affection and his sensibility, and
ended by inveighing against reason.   His perpetual refrain
was, that philosophy, knowledge acquired by reason, was
a vain illusion; that reason herself knew not whither she
led; that she but conducted mankind into a dark labyrinth
of error and contradiction; and that faith alone was their
sure guide.   Mole that he was, he saw not that reason,
like the eternal sun, whilst pursuing in the heavens an
appointed course, illumines its path with its own rays.
Nothing can compare with the fanatical hatred of the
little Jacobi towards the great Spinoza.

It is curious to observe how the most opposite parties
arrayed themselves against Spinoza.   The aspect of this
army of adversaries is highly amusing.   Near a swarm of
black and white Capuchins bearing cross and censer,
marches the phalanx of the Encyclopædists, who also
take aim at this "daring thinker" (*penseur temeraire*);
by the side of the Rabbi of the synagogue of Amsterdam,
who sounds the attack with the sacred buck's-horn, ad-
vances Arouet de Voltaire playing obligato on the shrill
pipe of irony for the benefit of deism; in the midst
whimpers the old woman Jacobi, the sutler of this army
of the faith.

Let us escape as quickly as possible from this charivari.
Returning from our pantheistic excursion we come back
to the Leibnitzian philosophy, of whose ulterior destiny in
Germany we have now to speak.

In writing his works, which are familiar to you,
Leibnitz employed partly the Latin and partly the French
language.   Christian Wolf is the name of the admirable
man who not only systematically taught the ideas of
Leibnitz, but did so in the German language.   His real
merit consists not in having formulated Leibnitzian ideas in
a solid system, still less does it consist in rendering them
accessible to a wider public by translation into German:

his special merit lies in having incited us to philosophise in our mother-tongue. Till Luther's time we were unable to treat of theology except in Latin ; till the time of Wolf we were obliged to philosophise in that language. The example of a few rare scholars, who had previously essayed to teach such subjects in German, led to no result. Yet the literary historian must accord to these few a special eulogy. In particular, we recall John Tauler,[7] a Dominican monk, who was born at the beginning of the fourteenth century on the banks of the Rhine, and died at Strasburg in 1361. He was a pious man, one of that body of mystics whom I have designated the Platonic party of the Middle Ages. In the last years of his life this man, renouncing all pride of learning, was not ashamed to preach in the humble language of the people ; and these sermons, which he committed to writing, as well as German translations of some of his former homilies in Latin, are to be reckoned amongst the monuments of the German language. For this language already proved itself not only appropriate for metaphysical investigations, but also far better adapted for this purpose than Latin. This latter, the language of the Romans, can never belie its origin. It is a language of command for generals ; a language of decree for administrators ; an attorney language for usurers ; a lapidary speech for the stone-hard Roman people. It became the appropriate language of Materialism. Though Christianity, with true Christian patience, tormented itself for more than a thousand years with the attempt to spiritualise this tongue, its efforts remained fruitless ; and when John Tauler sought to fathom the awful abysses of thought, and his heart overflowed with religious emotion, he was impelled to speak German. His speech is like a mountain spring that wells forth from the granite rock, marvellously impregnated with strange aroma and mysterious metallic virtues. It was not, however, till recent times that the rare appropriateness of German for philosophic purposes became fully apparent. In no other language than in our dear German mother-tongue could Nature have revealed her most intimate secret. Only on the robust oak can the sacred mistletoe thrive.

This would indeed be the fitting place to speak of Paracelsus, or, as he styled himself, Aureolus Theophrastus Paracelsus Bombastus of Hohenheim; for he also wrote chiefly in German. But I shall have occasion to speak of him later on from a still more important standpoint. His philosophy was what in our day we call the Philosophy of Nature ; and this doctrine of a nature animated by ideas, so mysteriously according with the spirit of German thought, would have taken root amongst us in the time of Paracelsus, had not the lifeless and mechanical theories of the Cartesians, through foreign influence, usurped universal authority.   Paracelsus was a great charlatan, always tricked himself out in scarlet coat and breeches, red stockings and a red hat, and asserted that he had power to create little men, *homunculi ;* at any rate he stood on the most familiar footing with the invisible beings that people the various elements. Yet he was also one of the profoundest of naturalists, who, with an ardour for investigation altogether German, comprehended pre-Christian popular beliefs, German pantheism, and what he did not know he very accurately divined.

Of Jacob Böhme I ought also to say something. He too applied the German language to philosophical demonstrations, for which he has been much praised. But I have never yet been able to bring myself to read his works. I do not like being made a fool of. I have, in fact, a suspicion that the panegyrists of this mystic have a desire to mystify the public. As regards the nature of his speculations, Saint Martin has given you a taste in French. In England also his works have been translated. Charles I. had so high an opinion of this theosophical shoemaker that he sent expressly a man of learning to Görlitz in order to study him. This learned man was more fortunate than his royal master; for whilst the latter lost his head at Whitehall under Cromwell's axe, the former merely lost his reason at Görlitz through the theosophy of Jacob Böhme.[8]

As I have said, Christian Wolf first successfully applied the German language to philosophy. His least merit was the reducing to a system and the popularising of Leibnitzian ideas. In both of these respects he has incurred the gravest censure, a censure that must not be passed over in silence. His systematising was merely a deceptive appearance and the most important element of the philosophy of Leibnitz—the best part of the theory of monads —was sacrificed to this appearance. Leibnitz had, it is true, left behind him no systematic edifice, only the necessary ideas towards its construction. It needed the might of a giant to fit together the colossal blocks and columns that a giant had raised from the deep marble quarries of thought and had hewn into symmetrical form. The result might have been a magnificent temple; but Christian Wolf was far too short of stature, and was unable to possess himself of more than a portion of the materials, with which he patched together a miserable tabernacle of deism. Wolf's intellect was more encyclopædic than systematic; he could not comprehend the unity of a doctrine except as a completed whole. He was content with the construction of a cabinet in which the compartments were arranged in the most orderly manner, conveniently filled, and legibly ticketed. In this way he has given us an Encyclopædia of Philosophical Sciences. As descended from Descartes through Leibnitz, it is easy to understand that he inherited from his grandfather the mathematical form of demonstration. I have already reprobated this mathematical form in Spinoza. In the hands of Wolf it became a source of great mischief; amongst his disciples it degenerated into insufferable methodising and a ludicrous mania for demonstrating everything in mathematical fashion. Thus arose the so-called dogmatism of Wolf. All profound investigation ceased and was replaced by wearisome zeal for perspicuity; the philosophy of Wolf became more and more aqueous and finally inundated all Germany. The traces of this deluge are visible even down to our own day, and here and there on our most sterile academical summits may still be found old fossils of the Wolfian school.

Christian Wolf was born at Breslau in 1679, and died at Halle in 1754. His intellectual supremacy in German lasted during more than half a century. His relation to German theologians deserves special attention, and a notice of it forms the complement to our sketch of the fate of Lutheranism.

No field in the whole history of the Church is more perplexing than the quarrels of Protestant theologians since the Thirty Years' War. They can only be compared with the puerile wranglings of the Byzantines. Yet the latter were less wearisome, for behind them were concealed political interests and court intrigues, whereas Protestant polemics were traceable, for the most part, to the pedantry of narrow-minded dons and freshmen. The universities, especially Tübingen, Wittenberg, Leipzic, and Halle, are the arenas of these theological combats. The two parties, whom we have seen contending in Catholic costume throughout the entire Middle Ages—the Platonists and the Aristotelians—have merely changed their mode of dress, and continue to wrangle as before. These are the pietists and the orthodox, of whom I have already spoken, and whom I designated as mystics without imagination and as dogmatists without intelligence. Philipp Jakob Spener* was the Scotus Erigena of Protestantism; and as the latter, by his translation of the legendary Dionysius the Areopagite, became the founder of Catholic mysticism, the former by his Conventicles for Edification, *Collegia pietatis,* from which, perhaps, the name "Pietists" still remains amongst his followers, founded Protestant pietism. He was a godly man,—reverence be to his memory. A Berlin Pietist, F. Horn, has written an excellent biography of him. The life of Spener was an incessant martyrdom for the Christian idea. In this respect he was preeminent among his contemporaries. He enforced the merits of godliness and good works; he was a preacher of the spirit rather than of the word. His homilies are very laudable, considering his time; for, all theology, as taught in the universities just mentioned, consisted in mere strait-laced dogmatism and hair-splitting polemic : exegesis and the study of Church history were completely ignored.

One of Spener's pupils, Hermann Franke, began to lecture at Leipzic after the example and method of his teacher. He read in German, a merit we are always ready to acknowledge with gratitude. The approbation with which these lectures were received excited the envy of his colleagues, and thus caused much bitterness in the life of our poor Pietist. Obliged to quit the field, he betook himself to Halle, where he taught Christianity by word and deed. His memory is there imperishable, for he was the founder of the Orphan Institute of Halle. The university of Halle soon became the headquarters of the

* In all the German editions, and even in the latest edition of the French version, the founder of the Pietists is erroneously called *Johannes* Spener. Heine had frequent occasion to complain of the careless manner in which his works were printed ; and his letters to Campe, the publisher, are full of reproaches on the subject. *Collegia pietatis* is transformed in all the editions into *Colloquia pietatis.*—TR.

Pietists, who were called "the Sect of the Orphanage" ("*Waisenhauspartei*"). Let it be said, in passing, that this sect flourishes there till the present day; Halle is still the mole-hill of the Pietists, whose quarrels with the rationalist Protestants created but a few years ago a scandal that became noised abroad throughout the whole of Germany. Happy Frenchmen, who have heard nothing of all this! You have remained ignorant of even the existence of those tattling evangelical journals in which the pious fishwives of the Protestant Church so lustily abused one another. Happy Frenchmen, who can form no idea of the malice, the pettiness, the bitterness with which our evangelical clergy can traduce one another! You know that I am no partisan of Catholicism. In the present state of my religious convictions there still survives, not indeed the dogmatism, but the spirit of Protestantism.* I still retain, therefore, my partiality for the Protestant Church; and yet must I honestly confess that nowhere in the annals of the Papacy have I discovered anything so contemptible as might be found in "The Berlin Evangelical Church Record" during the progress of this quarrel. The most dastardly knavery of the monks, the meanest intrigues of the cloister, are noble and generous compared to the Christian exploits of our pietist and orthodox Protestants during their combat with the hated Rationalists. You Frenchmen have no idea of the hatred

---

* In the French version the following is substituted for this sentence :—" Protestantism was for me more than a religion, it was a mission ; and for fourteen years I have been fighting in its interests against the machinations of the German Jesuits. My sympathy for dogma has, it is true, of late become extinguished, and I have frankly declared in my writings that my whole Protestantism consists in the fact that I was inscribed as an evangelical Christian in the church registers of the Lutheran communion. But a secret predilection for the cause in which we formerly fought and suffered always continues to nestle in our hearts, and my present religious convictions are still animated by the spirit of Protestantism."—Tr.

that is displayed on such occasions; for the Germans are more vindictive than the peoples of Latin origin. The reason is, they are idealists even in their hatred. We do not hate each other as you French do about outward things, because of wounded vanity, on account of an epigram, or of an unreturned visiting-card; no, we hate in our enemies the deepest, most vital possession they have, their thought. As in your love so in your hatred, you French are hasty, superficial. We Germans hate thoroughly, lastingly. Too honest, perhaps too unskilful, to revenge ourselves by speedy perfidy, we hate till our last breath. "I have had experience, sir, of this German tranquillity," said a lady to me not long ago, regarding me at the same time with a look of open-eyed incredulity and horror; "I know that in your language you employ the same word for begging pardon and for poisoning." And indeed she was right, the word *vergeben* has this twofold meaning.

It was, if I mistake not, the orthodox of Halle who, in their disputes with the Pietist refugees, called to their assistance the philosophy of Wolf; for religion when it can no longer burn us comes to beg from us an alms. Yet all our gifts profit it but little. The mantle of mathematical demonstration in which Wolf affectionately invested poor Religion fitted her so badly that she felt more straitened than before, and made herself very ridiculous through her discomfort. Weak seams gave way at all points. Original sin especially showed itself in its most glaring nakedness. No logical fig-leaf could avail it anything. Christian-Lutheran original sin and Leibnitz-Wolfian optimism are incompatible. French persiflage, at the expense of optimism, was therefore the least displeasing to our theologians. Voltaire's wit came to the aid of original sin, but the German Pangloss lost much by the overthrow of optimism, and he searched long for a doctrine equally consoling until the Hegelian axiom, " All that is, is reasonable!" afforded him some slight compensation.

From the moment that a religion solicits the aid of philosophy its ruin is inevitable. In the attempt at defence it prates itself into destruction. Religion, like every absolutism, must not seek to justify itself. Prometheus is bound to the rock by a silent force. Yea, Æschylus permits not personified power to utter a single word. It must remain mute. The moment that a religion ventures to print a catechism supported by arguments, the moment that a political absolutism publishes an official newspaper, both are near their end. But therein consists our triumph: we have brought our adversaries to speech, and they must reckon with us.

It is certainly indisputable that religious, as well as political, absolutism has found powerful organs of expressions. Still do not let this alarm us. If the word lives, it may be carried by dwarfs; if it is dead, no giant can hold it upright.

Now, as I have just said, since Religion took to seeking aid from philosophy, German scholars, besides the providing of new garments, have made all sorts of experiments with her. They conceived the idea of bestowing on her a new youth, and they attempted this somewhat after the manner of Medea with the old king Æson. First a vein was opened and all superstitious blood allowed to trickle slowly out. To speak without metaphor, an endeavour was made to empty Christianity of all historical content, and thus leave nothing but morality. By this process Christianity was reduced to pure deism. Christ ceased to be co-regent with God; he was in a sense mediatised, and only as a private person did becoming reverence continue to be paid him. His moral character was extolled beyond measure, nor could eulogy strong enough be found to express what an excellent man he must have been. As regards the miracles he wrought, they were either explained according to physical theories, or people made as little to do as possible about them. Miracles, said some, were necessary in those superstitious times, and a sensible man having a truth of any kind to proclaim, made use of miracles as an advertisement. Those theologians that sought entirely to eliminate the historical element from Christianity were called Rationalists. and upon them was poured out the wrath alike of Pietists and of the Orthodox. These sects are now less hostile to one another, and frequently even become confederates. What Christian love could not do was effected by a common hatred—hatred towards the Rationalists.

This tendency in Protestant theology * began with the peaceful Semler, whom you do not know, rose to a disquieting height with the clear-sighted Teller, whom also you do not know, and reached its culminating point with the shallow-brained Bahrdt, in the loss of whose acquaintance you have nothing to regret. The strongest impetus came from Berlin, where ruled Frederick the Great, and bookseller Nicolai.

As regards the first—crowned Materialism—you are sufficiently informed. You know that he composed French verses, played very well on the flute, won the battle of Rossbach, was a prodigious snuffer, and believed in nothing but cannon. Some of you have doubtless visited Sans-Souci, and the old pensioner who attends at the castle has pointed out to you in the library the French novels which Frederick when crown prince used to read in church, and which he caused to be bound in black morocco in order that his stern father might suppose him to be reading the Lutheran hymnal. Ye know him, that royal worldly-wise-man, whom you have named the Solomon of the North. France was the Ophir of this northern

* The French version has, " This reform of Protestant theology."—Tr.

Solomon, whence he obtained his poets and philosophers, for whom he cherished great favour, just like the Solomon of the South, who, as we read in the tenth chapter of the First Book of Kings, got his friend Hiram to bring from Ophir whole shiploads of gold and silver, ivory, poets, and philosophers.* This preference for foreign talent certainly hindered Frederick the Great from gaining any considerable influence over the German spirit. On the contrary, he insulted and wounded German national feeling. The contempt shown by him for our literature cannot but offend us the descendants of these writers. Except old Gellert none of them had reason to enjoy any mark of Frederick's most gracious favour. Gellert's interview with him is remarkable.

But if Frederick the Great jeered at us without offering to protect us, so much the more did we receive the protection of bookseller Nicolai, without having on that account any scruple about scoffing at him. This man was during his whole life incessantly active for the welfare of his country. He spared neither money nor pains where he hoped to further a good cause; and yet never has any one in Germany been so cruelly, so unrelentingly, so utterly ridiculed as this same man. Although we, the later-born, know right well that old Nicolai, the friend of enlightenment, was in the main in the right; though we know that it was chiefly our own enemies, the Obscurantists, that quizzed him to death, yet we cannot think of him with perfectly grave faces. Old Nicolai tried to do in Germany what the French philosophers had done in France: he endeavoured to destroy the past in

---

* In the French version Heine here quotes the Vulgate : " Classis regis per mare cum classe Hiram semel per tres annos ibat, deferens inde aurum et argentum, et dentes elephantorum, et simias et pavos." For the "apes and peacocks," sought after by the wise king, Heine substitutes (French) "poets and philosophers."—TR.

the spirit of the people ; a praiseworthy preparatory task, without which no radical revolution is possible. But in vain ; he was not robust enough for such a labour. The old ruins still stood too securely, and the phantom of the past arose out of them, and mocked his efforts ; then, losing his temper, he struck blindly at them, and the spectators laughed as the bats whizzed about his ears and got entangled in his powdered wig. Sometimes it happened that he mistook windmills for giants, and valiantly attacked them. But it fared worse with him when he mistook real giants for windmills,—a Wolfgang Goethe for example. He wrote a satire on *Werther* in which he utterly misapprehended its author's intentions. Yet, after all, he was right in the main. If he did not exactly understand Goethe's real object in *Werther*, he at least comprehended very clearly the tendency of that work— the effeminate dreaminess, the barren sentimentality it brought into vogue, which were in complete contradiction to every rational feeling of which we stood in need. Here Nicolai was entirely at one with Lessing, who wrote to a friend the following estimate of *Werther :*—

" In order that such an impassioned production may not be the means of producing more evil than good, do you not think it should have been provided with a short but very chilling epilogue, a few hints as to the causes that produced in Werther such a strange character, a contrast with some other young man on whom nature had bestowed a like temperament but who has power to over-rule it ? Do you suppose that a Greek or Roman youth would ever have killed himself in such a manner and from the same cause ? Assuredly not. The latter knew how to protect themselves in quite a different fashion from the extravagancies of love. It was reserved for Christianity, which can so beautifully transform a physical necessity into a spiritual perfection, to give birth to

eccentricities at once so mean and so great, so contemptible and so estimable. And so, dear Goethe, let us
have a short concluding chapter, and the more cynical
the better."

The worthy Nicolai has actually given us an edition of
Werther amended in accordance with this suggestion. In
this version the hero does not commit suicide, but only
smudges himself with chicken blood; for the pistol,
instead of being charged with lead, is loaded with nothing
more deadly than a blood-clot. Werther renders himself
ridiculous, continues to live, marries Charlotte, in short,
ends even more tragically than in Goethe's original.

"The Universal German Library" was the name of the
journal founded by Nicolai, wherein he and his friends
did battle with superstition, the Jesuits, the court lackeys,
&c. It cannot be denied that many a blow aimed at
superstition unfortunately fell on poetry. It was thus,
for example, that Nicolai made war on the nascent enthusiasm for old German popular poetry, and in the main
here again he was right; for these songs, with all possible
excellences, contained many reminiscences that were
unseasonable; these old strains, the *ranz des vaches* of the
Middle Ages, had power to entice back the sensibilities of
people to the cowsheds of the past. Like Ulysses, he
tried to stop the ears of his companions that they might
not hear the song of the Syrens, heedless whether henceforth they remained deaf also to the innocent warbling of
the nightingale. In order radically to clear the soil of
the present from old weeds, this practical man concerned
himself little whether with the weeds he also uprooted
the flowers. But the party of the flowers and the nightingales, with all that belonged to that party, beauty, grace,
wit, and pleasantry, indignantly rose up against him, and
poor Nicolai had to succumb.

In our day circumstances in Germany are changed, and

the party of the flowers and the nightingales is intimately allied with the revolution. The future belongs to us, and already the rosy morn of victory begins to dawn. If ever this beautiful day should shed its light over the whole Fatherland, then shall we call to mind the dead; we shall think of thee too, old Nicolai, poor martyr of reason! We shall bear thy ashes to the German pantheon in the midst of a triumphant procession accompanied by a choir of music, and amongst the wind instruments shall certainly be no shrill fife; we shall lay upon thy bier a befitting crown of laurel, and as we perform this act we shall do our utmost not to smile.

As it is my desire to give an idea of the philosophic and religious condition of those times, I must here refer to the thinkers who laboured at Berlin in more or less intimate association with Nicolai, and who occupied a sort of mean between philosophy and polite literature. They had no special system, only a special tendency. They resembled the English moralists as to their style and in their first principles. They wrote without observing strict scientific form; and moral consciousness was the sole origin of their knowledge. Their tendency is precisely that which we find in the French philanthropists. In religion they are rationalists, in politics cosmopolitans; in morals they are men, noble and virtuous men, severe towards themselves, indulgent towards others. In respect of talent, Mendelssohn, Sulzer, Abt, Moritz, Garve, Engel, and Biester may be named as the most distinguished amongst them. I have a peculiar liking for Moritz; he did good service in experimental psychology; his artlessness was charming, though but little appreciated by his friends; his memoirs form one of the most remarkable landmarks of the time. Mendelssohn,* however, has a social significance far be-

---

* For what is by far the best account of Moses Mendelssohn ac- cessible to English readers, we are indebted to " German Life and Lite-

yond all the others. He was the reformer of the German Israelites, his co-religionists; he destroyed the authority of the Talmud; he founded pure Mosaïsm. This man, whom his contemporaries called the German Socrates, and whom they so reverently admired for his nobility of soul and force of intellect, was the son of a poor sacristan of the synagogue at Dessau. In addition to this misfortune of birth, Providence sent him into the world hunchbacked, as if to teach the rabble in a striking manner that men are to be judged, not by their external appearance, but by their intrinsic worth. Or, did Providence allot him a hunchback in order that he might ascribe many an insult of the rabble to a misfortune for which a wise man readily consoles himself ?

As Luther had overthrown the Papacy, so Mendelssohn overthrew the Talmud; and he did so after the same fashion, namely, by rejecting tradition, by declaring the Bible to be the source of religion, and by translating the most important part of it. By these means he shattered Judaic, as Luther had shattered Christian, catholicism; for the Talmud is, in fact, the catholicism of the Jews. It is a Gothic cathedral, overladen no doubt with childish and superfluous ornament, yet awakening our astonishment by its heaven-aspiring, gigantic proportions. It is a hierarchy of religious laws, often relating to the most fanciful and ridiculous subtilties, but so ingeniously superimposed and subordinated, each part sustaining and supporting another, and so terribly consistent as to form an awe-inspiring, colossal whole.

Christian catholicism once overthrown, the catholicism

rature in a Series of Biographical Studies," by Alexander Hay Japp, LL.D. Marshall, Japp, & Co., London. No better introduction to the study of modern German literature could be desired. Dr. Japp's book, besides accurate biography, contains much sound criticism, and the author's enthusiasm for his subject never betrays him into mere hero-worship.—TR.

of the Jews, the Talmud, must also succumb: for the
Talmud had henceforth lost its significance; it served
merely as a bulwark against Rome, and it enabled the
Jews to offer as heroic a resistance to Christian Rome
as formerly they had offered to Pagan Rome.   And they
have not only resisted; they have been victorious.   The
poor Rabbi of Nazareth over whose dying head the Pagan
Roman inscribed the scoffing words, "King of the Jews,"
even this King of the Jews in mockery, thorn-crowned
and clad in ironical purple, became at last the God of
the Romans, and before him they had to bend the knee!
As heathen Rome had been, so Christian Rome was vanquished and has even become tributary.   If you have a
mind, dear reader, to betake yourself on one of the first days
of the quarter to the Rue Laffitte, No. 15, you will there
see a lumbering carriage draw up before the high door-
way, and from it steps down a stout man.   He mounts a
staircase leading to a small room in which is seated a
younger fair-haired man, though he is really older than
he looks—a man with the distinguished, negligent air of
a grand seigneur, underlying which, however, there is
something so solid, so positive, so absolute, that he might
be thought to have all the world's wealth in his pocket.
And truly he has all the world's wealth in his pocket,
for his name is Mr. James Rothschild, and the stout man
is Monsignor Grimbaldi, legate of his holiness the Pope,
in whose name he brings the interest on the Roman loan,
the tribute of Rome.

Of what use, now, the Talmud?

Moses Mendelssohn, then, deserves the highest praise
for having destroyed in Germany, at any rate, Jewish
catholicism; for what is superfluous is injurious.   But in
rejecting tradition he endeavoured to maintain as a religious duty the Mosaic ceremonial law.   Was this timidity
or was it prudence?   Was it the sorrowful constraint of

lingering affection that forbade his laying destructive
hands on objects that had been the most sacred in the
eyes of his forefathers, and for which so much blood and
so many martyr tears had flowed? I do not believe it.
Like the sovereigns of material kingdoms, the sovereigns
of the spirit must harden their hearts against family affections; and on the throne of thought men dare not give
way to tender sensibilities. I am much rather of opinion
therefore that Moses Mendelssohn saw in pure Mosaïsm
an institution that might serve as a last intrenchment of
deism; for deism was his inmost faith, his most profound
conviction. When his friend Lessing died and was
accused of Spinozism, he defended him with the most
anxious zeal, and fretted himself to death over the accusation.

I have already, for the second time, mentioned a name
that no German can pronounce without waking in his
bosom an echo more or less loud. Since Luther, Germany
has produced no greater, no better man than Gotthold
Ephraim Lessing. These two men are our pride and our
joy. Amidst the gloom of this present time we look
upwards towards these consoling figures, and they beckon
to us with signs of glorious promise. Yea, the third man
will also come, who will complete what Luther began,
what Lessing carried forward, and of whom the German
Fatherland has such dire need, the third emancipator!
I see already the gleam of his golden armour shining
through his imperial purple mantle, like the sun through
the ruddy dawn!

Like Luther's, Lessing's work consisted not merely in
positive achievement, but in rousing to its very depths
the German nation, and in giving a beneficial impulse
to intellectual movement by his criticism and by his
polemic. Lessing was the living criticism of his time,
and his whole life was a polemic. His criticism made

itself felt throughout the whole range of thought and of feeling—in religion, in science, in art; his polemic overcame every adversary and waxed stronger with every victory. As he himself avowed, conflict was necessary to his mental development. He resembled the legendary Norman, who inherited the talents, the skill, and the vigour of the enemies slain by him in combat, and thus at last became endowed with every possible advantage and excellence. We may well suppose that such an unwearied champion caused no small stir in Germany, in that tranquil Germany where, in those days, an even greater Sabbath stillness reigned than in our time. The majority were struck dumb by such literary daring. But his hardihood stood Lessing in good stead; for *to dare* is the secret of success in literature as well as in revolution and in love. Lessing's sword inspired terror in every breast; no head was secure from its strokes. Yea, he struck off many a skull out of pure wantonness, and then was malicious enough to pick it up again and to show the public that it was quite empty. Him whom he could not reach with the sword of his logic he slew with the arrows of his wit. Friends admired the gay feathers with which his arrows were winged; enemies felt their points rankling in their breasts. Lessing's wit had nothing in common with that playfulness, that gaiety, those bounding sallies that Frenchmen so well know. His wit was no little French spaniel chasing its own shadow; it was more like a great German tomcat playing with a mouse before strangling it.

Polemic was truly Lessing's delight, and therefore he never considered very attentively whether his opponent was worthy of him. Thus it comes that by his polemic many a name has been snatched from well-merited oblivion. He has enveloped with the most spiritual irony, with the most delicious humour, not a few paltry scribblers, who are preserved for all future time in Lessing's works, like insects embedded in a piece of amber. In the act of putting his adversaries to death he has bestowed on them immortality. Who amongst us would ever have heard anything of that Klotz on whom Lessing lavished so much derision and acumen? The granite blocks that he hurled down upon this miserable antiquary, and with which he crushed him to atoms, form an indestructible monument to the object of his satire.

It is remarkable that this man, the most redoubtable wit in Germany, was also our most honest man. There is nothing comparable to his love of truth. He would not grant the slightest concession to a lie, even though by doing so, after the manner of the wise men of the world, he might promote the triumph of truth. He dared do everything for the truth except lie. Whoever, he once said, supposes that he may bring truth to market under all sorts of artifices and disguises, may indeed be the pander, but he has never been the lover, of truth.

The admirable saying of Buffon, "The style is the man himself," finds in Lessing its best exemplification. His manner of writing is, like his character, truthful, firm, without ornament, beautiful and imposing by reason of inherent strength. His style is altogether like that of Roman architecture; it combines the greatest solidity with greatest simplicity; the sentences rest one upon another like blocks of square-hewn masonry. As for the latter the law of gravity, so in Lessing's writings logical sequence, is the invisible binding power. In his prose, therefore, there are but few of those redundancies and artificial turns of expression which we employ as mortar in the construction of our periods. Still less do we find in it any of those caryatides of thought which you French call *la belle phrase.*

That such a man as Lessing could never be happy you will readily understand. Even though he had not loved truth, though he had not obstinately defended it on all occasions, he would still have been unhappy, for he was a genius. Men will forgive you everything, said a poet lately, with a sigh: they will forgive you wealth, they will forgive you noble birth, they will forgive you a handsome form, they will even admit that you are talented; but they are inexorable in their enmity towards genius. And alas! even though it encounter no malignant enemy from without, genius will be sure to find within itself an enemy ready to bring calamity upon it. This is why the history of great men is always a martyrology; when they are not sufferers for the great human race, they suffer for their own greatness, for the grand manner of their being, for their hatred of philistinism, for the discomfort they feel amidst the pretentious commonplaces, the mean trivialities of their surroundings—a discomfort that readily leads them to extravagances, to the playhouse, for example, or even to the gambling-house, as happened to poor Lessing.

But evil rumour could find no other reproach to lay to his charge than this, and all we learn from his biography on the subject is, that pretty actresses seemed to him more amusing than Hamburg clergymen, and that mute cards afforded him better entertainment than the prating of Wolfian philosophers.

It is heartrending to read in his biography how fate denied this man every source of joy, and would not even permit him to find solace in the peace of family life at the close of his daily conflicts. Once only did fortune appear desirous of smiling on him by bestowing on him a beloved wife and a child. Yet this joy was but as the sunbeam that gilds the wing of a bird in passing flight. Even as quickly did it disappear. His wife died from the effects of her confinement, and his child immediately after its birth. Of his child he wrote to a friend those words of bitter irony :—

" My joy was but brief, and I lost him with such regret, this son! For he showed so much intelligence—so much intelligence! Do not suppose that my few hours of paternity had already made me an ape of a father. I know what I say. Did it not show intelligence on his part that they had to bring him into the world by means of iron forceps, and that he so quickly perceived what a troublous world it is? Was it not intelligence that caused him to seize the first opportunity of making his escape out of it again? I too wanted for once to be as highly favoured as other men; but I have come badly out of it."

There was one misfortune about which Lessing never spoke to his friends: this was his terrible isolation, his intellectual solitariness. A few of his contemporaries loved him; none understood him. Mendelssohn, his dearest friend, defended him with zeal against the charge of Spinozism. Defence and zeal were as ridiculous as they were superfluous. Rest in peace in thy grave, old Moses! Thy Lessing was indeed on the highroad towards that dreadful heresy, that pitiful misfortune called Spinozism; but the Almighty, the Father in heaven, saved him through death at the right moment. Rest in peace! thy Lessing was no Spinozist, as calumny asserted; he died a good deist, like thyself, and Nicolai, and Teller, and " The Universal German Library "!

Lessing was but the prophet pointing out the way from the second to the third Testament. I have called him the continuator of Luther, and it is specially in this relation that I have now to speak of him. Of his importance as influencing German art I shall afterwards deal. In art, not merely by his criticism but also by his example, he effected a wholesome reform, and this side of his activity is the one usually illustrated and brought into prominence. We, however, regard him from another standpoint, and his

philosophical and theological contests are of more importance to us than his dramaturgy and his dramas. Yet the
latter, like all his writings, have a social significance, and
"Nathan the Wise" is in reality not only a good comedy
but also a philosophico-theological treatise in favour of
pure deism. Art was for Lessing also a tribune, and when
thrust from the pulpit or driven from the philosopher's
chair, he sprang upon the boards of the theatre and spoke
there in still plainer language, and gained a still more
numerous audience.

I say that Lessing continued the work of Luther. After
Luther had emancipated us from the power of tradition
and set up the Bible as the only source of Christianity,
there arose a frigid literalism, and the letter of the Bible
became as great a tyranny as tradition had formerly been.
From this tyranny of the letter Lessing was our great
liberator. As Luther was certainly not alone in the
combat with tradition, so Lessing was not indeed the only,
though by far the most valiant, combatant of the letter.
It is in this conflict that his battle-cry resounds most
loudly; it is here that he wields his sword with most
vigorous delight, and it is a sword that flashes and slays.
But it is here also that he is most sorely beset by the
black phalanx, and in the midst of such straits he once
cried out:—

"*O sancta simplicitas!* But I have not yet come to the
place where the good man who thus exclaimed could utter
only this exclamation. (These were the words pronounced
at the stake by John Huss.) We must first be heard; we
must first be judged by those who can and will hear and
judge us.

"Oh, that *he* might do so, he whom I would most gladly
have as my judge! Luther! thou great misunderstood
man! and misunderstood by none more than by those ob-
stinate ones who, with thy shoes in their hand, clamorous

but indifferent, go jogging along the road thou hast opened for them! Thou hast redeemed us from the bondage of tradition: who shall redeem us from the more intolerable bondage of the letter? Who shall at length bring to us a Christianity such as thou wouldst teach to-day, such as Christ himself would teach?"

Yes, the letter, said Lessing, is the last husk that envelops Christianity, and only after its destruction will the spirit of Christianity stand revealed. This spirit, however, is nothing else than what the philosophy of Wolf undertook to demonstrate, what philanthropists feel in their hearts, what Mendelssohn found in Mosaïsm, what Freemasons have chanted, what poets have sung, what was in Lessing's day making itself felt under every variety of form throughout Germany—pure Deism.

Lessing died at Brunswick in 1781, misunderstood, hated, and decried. In the same year appeared at Königsberg Immanuel Kant's "Critique of Pure Reason." With this book (which through a singular delay did not become generally known till the close of the decade) there begins in Germany an intellectual revolution which offers the most striking analogies to the material revolution in France, and which must to the deeper thinkers appear of at least as great importance as the latter. It developed itself in the same phases, and between both revolutions there exists the most remarkable parallelism. On each side of the Rhine we see the same breach with the past; all respect for tradition is withdrawn. As here, in France, every privilege, so there, in Germany, every thought, must justify itself; as here, the monarchy, the keystone of the old social edifice, so there, deism, the keystone of the old intellectual *régime*, falls from its place.

Of this catastrophe, the 21st of January,* for deism, we shall speak in the concluding part of this volume.

* Louis XVI. was beheaded on the 21st of January 1793.—TR.

A peculiar awe, a mysterious piety, forbids our writing more to-day. Our heart is full of shuddering compassion : it is the old Jehovah himself that is preparing for death. We have known him so well from his cradle in Egypt, where he was reared among the divine calves and crocodiles, the sacred onions, ibises, and cats. We have seen him bid farewell to these companions of his childhood and to the obelisks and sphinxes of his native Nile, to become in Palestine a little god-king amidst a poor shepherd people, and to inhabit a temple-palace of his own. We have seen him later coming into contact with Assyrian-Babylonian civilisation, renouncing his all-too-human passions, no longer giving vent to fierce wrath and vengeance, at least no longer thundering at every trifle. We have seen him migrate to Rome, the capital, where he abjures all national prejudices and proclaims the celestial equality of all nations, and with such fine phrases establishes an opposition to the old Jupiter, and intrigues ceaselessly till he attains supreme authority, and from the Capitol rules the city and the world, *urbem et orbem.* We have seen how, growing still more spiritualised, he becomes a loving father, a universal friend of man, a benefactor of the world, a philanthropist; but all this could avail him nothing!

Hear ye not the bells resounding? Kneel down. They are bringing the sacraments to a dying god!

PART THIRD.

It is related that an English mechanician, who had already invented the most ingenious machines, at last took it into his head to construct a man; and that he succeeded. The work of his hands deported itself and acted quite like a human being; it even contained within its leathern breast a sort of apparatus of human sentiment, differing not greatly from the habitual sentiments of Englishmen; it could communicate its emotions by articulate sounds, and the noise of wheels in its interior, of springs and escapements, which was distinctly audible, reproduced the genuine English pronunciation. This automaton, in short, was an accomplished gentleman, and nothing was wanting to render it completely human except a soul. But the English mechanician had not the power to bestow on his work this soul, and the poor creature, having become conscious of its imperfection, tormented its creator day and night with supplication for a soul. This request, daily repeated with growing urgency, became at last so insupportable to the poor artist that he took to flight in order to escape from his own masterpiece. But the automaton also took the mail coach, pursued him over the whole continent, travelled incessantly at his heels, frequently overtook him, and then gnashed and growled in his ears, *Give me a soul!* These two figures may now be met with in every country, and he only who knows their peculiar relationship to each other can comprehend their unwonted haste and their haggard anxiety. But as soon as we are made aware of their strange relationship, we at once discover in them something of a general character; we see how one portion of the English people is becoming weary of its mechanical existence, and is demanding a soul, whilst the other portion, tormented by such a request, is driven about in all directions, and that neither of them can endure matters at home any longer.

The story is a terrible one. It is a fearful thing when the bodies we have created demand of us a soul; but it is a far more dreadful, more terrible, more awful thing when we have created a soul, to hear that soul demanding of us a body, and to behold it pursuing us with this demand. The thought to which we have given birth is such a soul, and it leaves us no rest until we have endowed it with a body, until we have given it sensible reality. Thought strives to become action, the word to become flesh, and, marvellous to relate, man, like God in the Bible, needs only to express his thought and the world takes form; there is light or darkness; the waters separate themselves from the dry land; or it may even be that wild beasts are brought forth. The world is the sign-manual of the word.

Mark this, ye proud men of action: ye are nothing but unconscious hodmen of the men of thought who, often in humblest stillness, have appointed you your inevitable task. Maximilian Robespierre was merely the hand of Jean Jacques Rousseau, the bloody hand that drew from the womb of time the body whose soul Rousseau had created. May not the restless anxiety that troubled the life of Jean Jacques have caused such stirrings within him that he already foreboded the kind of accoucheur that was needed to bring his thought living into the world ? *

Old Fontenelle may have been right when he said: " If

* This paragraph is wanting in the French version.—Tr.

I held all the truths of the universe in my hand, I would be very careful not to open it." I, for my part, think otherwise. If I held all the truths of the world in my hand, I might perhaps beseech you instantly to cut off that hand; but, in any case, I should not long hold it closed. I was not born to be a gaoler of thoughts; by Heaven! I would set them free. What though they were to incarnate themselves in the most hazardous realities, what though they were to range through all lands like a mad bacchanalian procession, what though they were to crush with their thyrsus our most innocent flowers, what though they were to invade our hospitals and chase from his bed the old sick world—my heart would bleed, no doubt, and I myself would suffer hurt thereby! For alas! I too am part of this old sick world, and the poet says truly, one may mock at his crutches yet not be able to walk any better for that. I am the most grievously sick of you all, and am the more to be pitied since I know what health is; but you do not know it, you whom I envy; you are capable of dying without perceiving your dying condition. Yea, many of you are already long since dead, though maintaining that your real life is just beginning. When I try to dispel such a delusion, then you are angry with me and rail at me, and, more horrible still, the dead rush upon and mock at me, and more loathsome to me than their insults is the smell of their putrefaction. Hence, ye spectres! I am about to speak of a man whose mere name has the might of an exorcism; I speak of Immanuel Kant.

It is said that night-wandering spirits are filled with terror at sight of the headsman's axe. With what mighty fear, then, must they be stricken when there is held up to them Kant's "Critique of Pure Reason"! This is the sword that slew deism in Germany.

To speak frankly, you French have been tame and moderate compared with us Germans. At most, you could but kill a king, and he had already lost his head before you guillotined him. For accompaniment to such deed you must needs cause such a drumming and shrieking and stamping of feet that the whole universe trembled. To compare Maximilian Robespierre with Immanuel Kant is to confer too high an honour upon the former. Maximilian Robespierre, the great citizen of the Rue Saint Honoré, had, it is true, his sudden attacks of destructiveness when it was a question of the monarchy, and his frame was violently convulsed when the fit of regicidal epilepsy was on; but as soon as it came to be a question about the Supreme Being, he wiped the white froth from his lips, washed the blood from his hands, donned his blue Sunday coat with silver buttons, and stuck a nosegay in the bosom of his broad vest.

The history of Immanuel Kant's life is difficult to portray, for he had neither life nor history. He led a mechanical, regular, almost abstract bachelor existence in a little retired street of Königsberg, an old town on the northeastern frontier of Germany. I do not believe that the great clock of the cathedral performed in a more passionless and methodical manner its daily routine than did its townsman, Immanuel Kant. Rising in the morning, coffee-drinking, writing, reading lectures, dining, walking, everything had its appointed time, and the neighbours knew that it was exactly half-past three o'clock when Immanuel Kant stepped forth from his house in his grey, tight-fitting coat, with his Spanish cane in his hand, and betook himself to the little linden avenue called after him to this day the " Philosopher's Walk." Summer and winter he walked up and down it eight times, and when the weather was dull or heavy clouds prognosticated rain, the townspeople beheld his servant, the old Lampe, trudging anxiously behind him with a big umbrella under his arm, like an image of Providence.

What a strange contrast did this man's outward life present to his destructive, world-annihilating thoughts! In sooth, had the citizens of Königsberg had the least presentiment of the full significance of his ideas, they would have felt a far more awful dread at the presence of this man than at the sight of an executioner, who can but kill the body. But the worthy folk saw in him nothing more than a Professor of Philosophy, and as he passed at his customary hour, they greeted him in a friendly manner and set their watches by him.

But though Immanuel Kant, the arch-destroyer in the realm of thought, far surpassed in terrorism Maximilian Robespierre, he had many similarities with the latter, which induce a comparison between the two men. In the first place, we find in both the same inexorable, keen, poesyless, sober integrity. We likewise find in both the same talent of suspicion, only that in the one it manifested itself in the direction of thought and was called criticism, whilst in the other it was directed against mankind and was styled republican virtue. But both presented in the highest degree the type of the narrow-minded citizen. Nature had destined them for weighing out coffee and sugar, but fate decided that they should weigh out other things, and into the scales of the one it laid a king, into the scales of the other a God. . . . And they both gave the correct weight!

The "Critique of Pure Reason" is Kant's principal work; and as none of his other writings is of equal importance, in speaking of it we must give it the right of preference. This book appeared in 1781, but, as already said, did not become generally known till 1789. At the time of its publication it was quite overlooked, except for two insignificant notices, and it was not till a later period that public attention was directed to this great book by the articles of Schütz, Schultz, and Reinhold. The cause of this tardy recognition undoubtedly lay in the unusual form and bad style in which the work is written. As regards his style, Kant merits severer censure than any other philosopher, more especially when we compare this with his former and better manner of writing. The recently published collection of his minor works contains his first attempts, and we are surprised to find in these an excellent and often very witty style. These little treatises were trilled forth while their author ruminated over his great work. There is a gleefulness about them like that of a soldier tranquilly arming for a combat in which he promises himself certain victory. Especially remarkable amongst them are his " Universal Natural History and Theory of the Heavens," composed as early as 1755 ; " Observations on the Emotions of the Sublime and Beautiful," written ten years later; and " Dreams of a Ghostseer," full of admirable humour after the manner of the French essay. Kant's wit as displayed in these pamphlets is of quite a peculiar sort. The wit clings to the thought, and in spite of its tenuity is thus enabled to reach a satisfactory height. Without such support wit, be it ever so robust, cannot be successful; like a vine-tendril wanting a prop, it can only creep along the ground to rot there with all its most precious fruits.

But why did Kant write his " Critique of Pure Reason " in such a colourless, dry, packing-paper style ? I fancy that, having rejected the mathematical form of the Cartesio-Leibnitzo-Wolfian school, he feared that science might lose something of its dignity by expressing itself in light, attractive, and agreeable tones. He therefore gave it a stiff, abstract form, which coldly repelled all familiarity on the part of intellects of the lower order. He wished haughtily to separate himself from the popular philosophers of his time, who aimed at the most citizen-like clearness, and so clothed his thoughts in a courtly and frigid official dialect. Herein he shows himself a true philistine. But it might also be that Kant needed for the carefully measured march of his ideas a language similarly precise, and that he was not in a position to create a better. It is only genius that has a new word for a new thought. Immanuel Kant, however, was no genius. Conscious of this defect, Kant, like the worthy Maximilian, showed himself all the more mistrustful of genius, and went so far as to maintain, in his "Critique of the Faculty of Judgment," that genius has no business with scientific thought, and that its action ought to be relegated to the domain of art.

The heavy, buckram style of Kant's chief work has been the source of much mischief; for brainless imitators aped him in his external form, and hence arose amongst us the superstition that no one can be a philosopher who writes well. The mathematical form, however, could not, after the days of Kant, reappear in philosophy; he has mercilessly passed sentence of death upon it in his "Critique of Pure Reason." The mathematical form in philosophy, he says, is good for nothing save the building of houses of cards, in the same way that the philosophic form in mathematics produces nothing but twaddle, for in philosophy there can be no definitions such as those in mathematics, where the definitions are not discursive but intuitive, that is to say, capable of being demonstrated by inspection; whilst what are called definitions in philosophy are only tentatively, hypothetically put forth, the real definition appearing only at the close, as result.

How comes it. that philosophers display so strong a predilection for the mathematical form? This predilection dates from the time of Pythagoras, who designated the principles of things by numbers. This was the idea of a genius: all that is sensible and finite is stripped off in a number, and yet it denotes something determined, and the relation of this thing to another determined thing, which last, designated in turn by a number, receives the same insensible and infinite character. In this respect numbers resemble ideas that preserve the same character and relation to one another. We can indicate by numbers in a very striking manner ideas, as they are produced in our mind and in nature; but the number still remains the sign of the idea, it is not the idea itself. The master is always conscious of this distinction, but the scholar forgets it, and transmits to other scholars at second hand merely a numerical hieroglyph, dead ciphers, which are repeated with parrot-like scholastic pride, but of which the living significance is lost. This applies likewise to the other methods of mathematical demonstration. The intellect in its eternal mobility suffers no arrest; and just as little can it be fixed down by lines, triangles, squares, and circles, as by numbers. Thought can neither be calculated nor measured.

As my chief duty is to facilitate in France the study of German philosophy, I always dwell most strongly on the external difficulties that are apt to dismay a stranger who has not already been made aware of them. I would draw the special attention of those who desire to make Frenchmen acquainted with Kant to the fact, that it is possible to abstract from his philosophy that portion which serves merely to refute the absurdities of the Wolfian philosophy. This polemic, constantly reappearing, will only tend to produce confusion in the minds of Frenchmen, and can be of no utility to them.

The "Critique of Pure Reason" is, as I have said, Kant's principal work, and his other writings are in a measure superfluous, or may at least be considered as commentaries. The social importance that attaches to his chief work will be apparent from what follows.

The philosophers who preceded Kant reflected, doubt-less, on the origin of our cognitions, and followed, as we have seen, two different routes, according to their view of ideas as *a priori* or as *a posteriori ;* but concerning the faculty of knowing, concerning the extent and limits of this faculty, they occupied themselves less. Now this was the task that Kant set before himself ; he submitted the faculty of knowing to a merciless investigation, he sounded all the depths of this faculty, he ascertained all its limits. In this investigation he certainly discovered that about many things, wherewith formerly we supposed ourselves to be most intimately acquainted, we can know nothing. This was very mortifying; but it has always been useful to know of what things we can know nothing. He who warns us against a useless journey performs as great a service for us as he who points out to us the true path. Kant proves to us that we know nothing about things as they are in and by themselves, but that we have a knowledge of them only in so far as they are reflected in our minds. We are therefore just like the prisoners of whose condition Plato draws such an afflicting picture in the seventh book of his Republic. These wretched beings, chained neck and thigh in such a manner that they cannot turn their heads about, are seated within a roofless prison, into which there comes from above a certain amount of light. This light, however, is the light from a fire, the flame of which rises up behind them, and indeed is separated from them only by a little wall. Along the outer side of this wall are walking men bearing all sorts of statues, images in wood and stone, and con-versing with one another. Now the poor prisoners can see nothing of these men, who are not tall enough to overtop the wall ; and of the statues, which rise above the wall, they see only the shadows flitting along the side of the wall opposite them. The shadows, however, they take for real objects, and, deceived by the echo of their prison, believe that it is the shadows that are conversing.

With the appearance of Kant former systems of philosophy, which had merely sniffed about the external aspect of things, assembling and classifying their characteristics, ceased to exist. Kant led investigation back to the human intellect, and inquired what the latter had to reveal. Not without reason, therefore, did he compare his philosophy to the method of Copernicus. Formerly, when men conceived the world as standing still, and the sun as revolving round it, astronomical calculations failed to agree accurately. But when Copernicus made the sun stand still and the earth revolve round it, behold! everything accorded admirably. So formerly reason, like the sun, moved round the universe of phenomena, and sought to throw light upon it. But Kant bade reason, the sun, stand still, and the universe of phenomena now turns round, and is illuminated the moment it comes within the region of the intellectual orb.

These few words regarding the task that presented itself to Kant will suffice to show that I consider that section of his book wherein he treats of *phenomena* and *noumena* as the most important part, as the central point, of his philosophy. Kant, in effect, distinguishes between the appearances of things and things themselves. As we can know nothing of objects except in so far as they manifest themselves to us through their appearance, and as objects do not exhibit themselves to us as they are in and by themselves, Kant gives the name *phenomena* to objects as they appear to us, and *noumena* to objects as they are in themselves. We know things, therefore, only as phenomena; we cannot know them as noumena. The latter are purely problematic; we can neither say that they exist nor that they do not exist. The word noumena has been correlated with the word phenomena merely to enable us to speak of things in so far as they are cognisable by us, without occupying our judgment about things that are not cognisable by us. Kant did not therefore, as do many teachers whom I will not name, make a distinction of objects into phenomena and noumena, into things that for us exist and into things that for us do not exist. This would be an Irish bull in philosophy. He wished merely to express a notion of limitation.

God, according to Kant, is a noumen. As a result of his argument, this ideal and transcendental being, hitherto called God, is a mere fiction.* It has arisen from a natural illusion. Kant shows that we can know nothing regarding this noumen, regarding God, and that all reasonable proof of his existence is impossible. The words of Dante, " Leave all hope behind ! " may be inscribed over this portion of the " Critique of Pure Reason."

My readers will, I think, gladly exempt me from attempting a popular elucidation of that portion of his work in which Kant treats " of the arguments of speculative reason in favour of the existence of a Supreme Being." Although the formal refutation of these arguments occupies but a small space, and is not taken in hand till the second part of the book is reached, there is already a very evident intention of leading up to this refutation, which forms one of the main points of the work. It connects itself with the " Critique of all Speculative Theology," wherein the last phantoms of deism are put to flight. I cannot help remarking that Kant, in attacking the three principal kinds of evidence in favour of the existence of God, namely, the ontological, the cosmological, and the physico-theological, whilst successful, according to my opinion, in refuting the latter two, fails with regard to the first. I am not aware whether the above terms are understood in this country, and I therefore quote the passage

* In the French version, " is only an assumption."—TR.

from the " Critique of Pure Reason" in which Kant for-
mulates the distinction between them.

" There are but three kinds of proof possible to speculative reason of the existence of God.   All the routes that
may be selected with this end in view start, either from
definite experience and the peculiar properties of the
external world, as revealed by experience, and ascend from
it according to the laws of causality up to the supreme
cause above the world ; or, they rest merely on an indefinite experience, as, for example, on an existence or being
of some kind or other; or, lastly, they make an abstraction
from all experience, and arrive at a conclusion entirely *a
priori* from pure ideas of the existence of the supreme
cause.   The first of these is the physico-theological proof,
the second the cosmological, and the third the ontological.
Other proofs there are none, nor can other proofs exist."

After repeated and careful study of Kant's chief work,
I fancied myself able to recognise everywhere visible in
it his polemic against these proofs of the existence of
God; and of this polemic I might speak at greater length
were I not restrained by a religious sentiment.   The mere
discussion by any one of the existence of God causes me
to feel a strange disquietude, an uneasy dread such as I
once experienced in visiting New Bedlam in London,
when, for a moment losing sight of my guide, I was surrounded by madmen.   " God is all that is," and doubt of
His existence is doubt of life itself, it is death.

The more blameworthy any dispute regarding the existence of God may be, the more praiseworthy is meditation
on the nature of God.   Such meditation is a true worship
of God; the soul is thereby detached from the perishable
and finite, and attains to consciousness of innate love and
of the harmony of the universe.   It is this consciousness
that sends a thrill through the heart of the emotional man
in the act of prayer or in the contemplation of the sacred

symbols; and the thinker realises this holy fervour in the exercise of that sublime faculty of the mind called reason, a faculty whose highest function is to inquire into the nature of God. Men of specially religious temperament concern themselves with this problem from childhood upwards; they are mysteriously troubled about it even at the first dawnings of reason.* The author of these pages is most joyfully conscious of having possessed this early primitive religious feeling, and it has never forsaken him. God was always the beginning and the end of all my thoughts. If I now inquire: What is God? what is his nature?—as a little child I had already inquired: How is God? what is he like? In that childish time I could gaze upwards at the sky during whole days, and was sadly vexed at evening because I never caught a glimpse of God's most holy countenance, but saw only the grey silly grimaces of the clouds. I was quite puzzled over the astronomical lore with which in the "enlighten-ment period" even the youngest children were tormented, and there was no end to my amazement on learning that all those thousand millions of stars were spheres as large and as beautiful as our own earth, and that over all this glitter-ing throng of worlds a single God ruled. I recollect once seeing God in a dream far above in the most distant firmament. He was looking contentedly out of a little window in the sky, a devout hoary-headed being with a small Jewish beard, and he was scattering forth myriads of seed-corns, which, as they fell from heaven, burst open in the infinitude of space, and expanded to vast dimen-sions till they became actual, radiant, blossoming, peopled worlds, each one as large as our own globe. I could never forget this countenance, and often in dreams I used to see the cheerful-looking old man sprinkling forth the

* The remainder of this paragraph, with the first two sentences of the succeeding one, is omitted in the French version.—TR.

world-seeds from his little window in the sky; once I even saw him clucking like our maid when she threw down for the hens their barley. I could only see how the falling seed-corns expanded into great shining orbs; but the great hens that may by chance have been waiting about with eager open bills to be fed with the falling orbs I could not see.

You smile, dear reader, at the notion of the big hens. Yet this childish notion is not so very different from the view of the most advanced deists. In the attempt to provide a conception of an extra-mundane God, orient and occident have exhausted themselves in hyperbole. The imagination of deists has, however, vainly tormented itself with the infinitude of time and space. It is here that their impotence, the inadequacy of their cosmology, and the untenableness of their explanation of the nature of God becomes fully apparent. We are not greatly distressed, therefore, at beholding the subversion of their explanation. Kant has actually wrought this affliction upon them by refuting their demonstration of the existence of God.

Nor would the vindication of the ontological proof specially benefit deism, for this proof is equally available for pantheism. To render my meaning more intelligible, I may remark that the ontological proof is the one employed by Descartes, and that long before his time, in the Middle Ages, Anselm of Canterbury had expressed it in the form of an affecting prayer. Indeed, St. Augustin may be said to have already made use of the ontological proof in the second book of his work, " De Libero Arbitrio."

I refrain, as I have said, from all popular discussion of Kant's polemic against these proofs. Let it suffice to give an assurance that since his time deism has vanished from the realm of speculative reason. It may, perhaps, be several centuries yet before this melancholy notice of decease gets universally bruited about; we, however, have long since put on mourning. *De Profundis!*

You fancy, then, that we may now go home! By my life, no! there is yet a piece to be played; after the tragedy comes the farce. Up to this point Immanuel Kant has pursued the path of inexorable philosophy; he has stormed heaven and put the whole garrison to the edge of the sword; the ontological, cosmological, and physico-theological bodyguards lie there lifeless; Deity itself, deprived of demonstration, has succumbed; there is now no All-mercifulness, no fatherly kindness, no other-world reward for renunciation in this world, the immortality of the soul lies in its last agony—you can hear its groans and death-rattle; and old Lampe is standing by with his umbrella under his arm, an afflicted spectator of the scene, tears and sweat-drops of terror dropping from his countenance. Then Immanuel Kant relents and shows that he is not merely a great philosopher but also a good man; he reflects, and half good-naturedly, half ironically, he says: "Old Lampe must have a God, otherwise the poor fellow can never be happy. Now, man ought to be happy in this world; practical reason says so;—well, I am quite willing that practical reason should also guarantee the existence of God." As the result of this argument, Kant distinguishes between the *theoretical reason* and the *practical reason,* and by means of the latter, as with a magician's wand, he revivifies deism, which theoretical reason had killed.

But is it not conceivable that Kant brought about this resurrection, not merely for the sake of old Lampe, but through fear of the police? Or did he act from sincere conviction? Was not his object in destroying all evidence for the existence of God to show us how embarrassing it might be to know nothing about God? In doing so, he acted almost as sagely as a Westphalian friend of mine, who smashed all the lanterns in the Grohnder Street in Göttingen, and then proceeded to deliver to us in the dark a long lecture on the practical necessity of lanterns, which he had theoretically broken in order to show how, without them, we could see nothing.

I have already said that on its appearance the " Critique of Pure Reason " did not cause the slightest sensation, and it was not till several years later, after certain clear-sighted philosophers had written elucidations of it, that public attention was aroused regarding the book. In the year 1789, however, nothing else was talked of in Germany but the philosophy of Kant, about which were poured forth in abundance commentaries, chrestomathies, interpretations, estimates, apologies, and so forth. We need only glance through the first philosophic catalogue at hand, and the innumerable works having reference to Kant will amply testify to the intellectual movement that originated with this single man. In some it exhibited itself as an ardent enthusiasm, in others as an acrid loathing, in many as a gaping curiosity regarding the result of this intellectual revolution. We had popular riots in the world of thought, just as you had in the material world, and over the demolition of ancient dogmatism we grew as excited as you did at the storming of the Bastille. There was also but a handful of old pensioners left for the defence of dogmatism, that is, the philosophy of Wolf. It was a revolution, and one not wanting in horrors. Amongst the party of the past, the really good Christians showed least indignation at these horrors. Yea, they desired even greater, in order that the measure of iniquity might be full, and the counter-revolution be more speedily accomplished as a necessary reaction. We had pessimists in philosophy as you had in politics. As in France there were people who maintained that Robespierre was the agent of Pitt, with us there were many who went so far in their wilful blindness as to persuade themselves that Kant was in secret alliance with them, and that he had destroyed all philosophic proofs of the existence of God merely in order to convince the world that man can never arrive at a knowledge of God by the help of reason, and must therefore hold to revealed religion.

Kant brought about this great intellectual movement less by the subject-matter of his writings than by the critical spirit that pervaded them, a spirit that now began to force its way into all sciences. It laid hold of all constituted authority. Even poetry did not escape its influence. Schiller, for example, was a strong Kantist, and his artistic views are impregnated with the spirit of the philosophy of Kant. By reason of its dry, abstract character, this philosophy was eminently hurtful to polite literature and the fine arts. Fortunately it did not interfere in the art of cookery.

The German people is not easily set in motion; but let it be once forced into any path and it will follow it to its termination with the most dogged perseverance. Thus we exhibited our character in matters of religion, thus also we now acted in philosophy. Shall we continue to advance as consistently in politics?

Germany was drawn into the path of philosophy by Kant, and philosophy became a national cause. A brilliant troop of great thinkers suddenly sprang up on German soil, as if called into being by magical art. If German philosophy should some day find, as the French revolution has found, its Thiers and its Mignet, its history will afford as remarkable reading as the works of these authors. Germans will study it with pride, and Frenchmen with admiration.

Among the followers of Kant, John Gottlieb Fichte soon rose into pre-eminence.

I almost despair of being able to convey an accurate impression of this man. In the case of Kant we had merely a book to examine; but here, besides the book, we have to take account of the man. In this man thought and purpose are one, and in this splendid unity they affect the contemporary world. We have therefore to investigate not a philosophy merely, but also the type by which that philosophy is conditioned, and in order thoroughly to comprehend this twofold influence we should have to pass in review the situation of this epoch. What a wide-reaching task! We shall, no doubt, be readily excused for offering merely an imperfect outline.

At the outset there is the greatest difficulty in stating explicitly the nature of Fichte's ideas. We have here to encounter peculiar obstacles, obstacles connected not only with the subject - matter but also with the form and method of its presentation—two things with which we are specially desirous of making foreigners acquainted. Let us begin, then, with the method of Fichte. At first he borrowed the method of Kant, but it soon underwent a change, resulting from the nature of the subject. Kant had merely to produce a critique, that is to say, something negative; whilst Fichte had by and by to develop a system, that is, something positive. This want of a definite system in the philosophy of Kant was the reason why it was sometimes refused the name philosophy. As regards Immanuel Kant himself, there was justice in this; but not as regards the Kantists, who constructed from Kant's propositions quite a sufficient number of definite systems. In his earlier writings, Fichte remained, as I have said, quite faithful to the method of his master, so much so that his first treatise, which was published anonymously, was attributed to Kant. But when Fichte afterwards produced a system he was seized with an ardent and persistent passion for construction, and after constructing the universe he sets about demonstrating, in all its aspects, with the same ardour and persistency, that which he has constructed. Whether constructing or demonstrating, Fichte manifests, so to speak, an abstract passion. As in his system, so, soon afterwards in his exposition, subjectivity is dominant. Kant, on the other hand, stretches out thought before him, analyses it, dissects it down to its minutest fibrils, and his " Critique of Pure Reason " is a kind of anatomical theatre of the human intellect; he himself, however, stands by, cold and insensible, like a true surgeon.

The form of Fichte's writings resembles his method; it is living, but it has also all the faults of life: it is restless and confused. That he may always remain thoroughly animated, Fichte disdains the customary terminology of philosophers, which seems to him a dead thing; but the effect of this is to make him still less comprehensible. About intelligibility in general he had quite a peculiar caprice. As long as Reinhold was of the same opinion with him, Fichte declared that no one understood him better than Reinhold. But when the latter differed from him in opinion, Fichte declared that he had never been understood by him. When he himself took a different view from Kant, he had it put in print that Kant did not understand himself. I am here touching upon the comical aspect of our philosophers, who are perpetually lamenting that they are misunderstood. When Hegel was lying on his deathbed, he said: " Only one man has understood me," but shortly afterwards he added fretfully: " And even he did not understand me."

Considered as to its substance, its intrinsic value, the philosophy of Fichte is of no great significance. It has afforded society no result. Only in so far as it exhibits above all other systems one of the most remarkable phases of German philosophy, only in so far as it attests the sterility of idealism in its last consequences, and only in so far as it forms the necessary transition to the philosophy of our day, does the substance of Fichte's doctrine possess a certain interest. This doctrine, being then of more importance in an historical and scientific than in a social aspect, I shall merely indicate it in a few words.

The question proposed by Fichte is, What grounds have we for assuming that our conceptions of objects correspond with objects external to us? And to this question he offers the solution: All things have reality only in our mind.

The "Critique of Pure Reason" was Kant's chief work, the "Theory of Knowledge"[9] was the chief work of Fichte. The latter book is a kind of continuation of the former. The "Theory of Knowledge" likewise refers the intellect back to itself. But where Kant analyses, Fichte constructs. The "Theory of Knowledge" opens with an abstract formula $(I = I)$; it re-creates the world out of the recesses of mind; it fits the disjointed parts together again; intelligence retraces its steps over the road it had travelled towards abstraction till it regains the world of phenomena. Thereafter reason is enabled to declare the phenomenal world to be a necessary operation of intelligence.

The philosophy of Fichte also presents the peculiar difficulty that it requires the mind to observe itself in the midst of its activity; the *Ego* is to investigate its own intellectual acts during the process of thinking; thought is to play the spy on itself whilst it thinks, whilst it grows gradually warmer until at last it is boiling. This operation reminds us of the monkey seated on the hearth before a copper kettle cooking its own tail; for it is of opinion that the true art of cookery consists not merely in the objective act of cooking, but also in the subjective consciousness of the process of cooking.

It is a singular circumstance that the philosophy of Fichte has always had to endure much from satire. I once saw a caricature representing a Fichtean goose. The poor bird has a liver so large that it no longer knows whether it is goose or liver. On its belly is inscribed *I-I.* Jean Paul has most wickedly quizzed the Fichtean philosophy in a book entitled *Clavis Fichteana.* That idealism pursued to its ultimate consequences should end by denying even the reality of matter seemed, to the great mass of the public, to be carrying the joke too far. We grew rather merry over the Fichtean Ego, which produced by its mere thinking the whole external world. The laughter of our wits was increased through a misapprehension that became too popular to permit of my passing it over in silence. The great mass really supposed that the *Ego* of Fichte was the Ego of Johann Gottlieb Fichte, and that this individual Ego implied a negation of all other existences. What an impertinence! exclaimed the worthy folk; this fellow does not believe that we exist, we who are much more corpulent than himself, and who, as burgomasters and bailiffs, are actually his superiors! The ladies inquired, Does he not at least believe in the existence of his wife? No! And Madam Fichte suffers this!

The Ego of Fichte, however, is not the individual but the universal Ego, the world-Ego awakened to self-consciousness. The Fichtean process of thought is not the thinking act of an individual, of a certain person called Johann Gottlieb Fichte; it is rather the universal thought manifesting itself in an individual. As we say, " It rains," " it lightens," and so on; so Fichte ought not to say, " I think," but, "it thinks," " the universal world-thought thinks in me."

In a parallel between the French revolution and German philosophy I once compared, more in jest than in earnest, Fichte to Napoleon. But there are, in fact, certain remarkable analogies between them. After the Kantists had accomplished their work of terrorism and destruction, Fichte appeared, as Napoleon appeared after the Convention had demolished the whole past by the help of another sort of Critique of Pure Reason. Napoleon and Fichte represent the great inexorable Ego for which thought and action are one; and the colossal structures raised by both men testify to a colossal will. But through the boundlessness of this will their structures soon fall to the ground, and both the "Theory of Knowledge" and the Empire crumble to pieces and disappear as quickly as they were reared.

The Empire is now nothing more than matter of history, but the commotion caused by the emperor in the world has not yet calmed down, and from this commotion our present Europe draws its vitality. It is the same with the philosophy of Fichte; it has completely perished, but men's minds are still agitated by the thoughts that found a voice in Fichte, and the after-effect of his teaching is incalculable. Even supposing all transcendental idealism to be an error, still the writings of Fichte are animated by a proud independence, by a love of liberty, by a virile dignity that have exercised, especially on the young, a wholesome influence. The Ego of Fichte was in complete accord with his inflexible, stubborn, stern character. The notion of an Ego so all-powerful could perhaps germinate only in such a character, and such a character intertwining its roots about such a doctrine could not but become more inflexible, more stubborn, more stern.

With what aversion must this man have been regarded by aimless sceptics, by frivolous ecclectics, and by moderates of all shades! His whole life was a combat. The story of his youth, like that of almost all our distinguished men, is the record of a series of afflictions. Poverty sits by their cradle and rocks them up to manhood, and this meagre nurse remains their faithful companion through life.

Nothing is more touching than the sight of the proud-willed Fichte struggling miserably through the world by the aid of tutorship. Nor can he obtain even thus the bitter bread of servitude in his own country, but has to migrate to Warsaw. There the old story repeats itself; the tutor displeases the gracious lady of the house, or perhaps only the ungracious lady's-maid. He cannot scrape a leg with sufficient gentility, is not French enough, and is no longer judged worthy to superintend the education of a young Polish squire. Johann Gottlieb Fichte is dismissed like a lackey, receives from his dissatisfied master hardly the meagre expenses of his journey, leaves Warsaw and betakes himself, full of youthful enthusiasm, to Königsberg, in order to make the acquaintance of Kant. The meeting of these two men is in every respect noteworthy. Perhaps I can present no clearer idea of their everyday life and circumstances than by citing a fragment from Fichte's journal, to be found in a biography of him, recently published by his son.*

"On the twenty-fifth of June I set out for Königsberg with a carrier of this town, and arrived there, without experiencing any remarkable incident, on the first of July. The fourth.—Visited Kant, who did not, however, receive me with any special distinction. I attended his lecture as an invited stranger, and again my expectation was disappointed. His delivery is drowsy. Meantime I have begun this journal.

"I have long felt a desire for a more serious interview with Kant, but could find no means of bringing this about. At last I hit upon the plan of writing a 'Critique of all

---

* "Fichte's Life and Literary Correspondence," by Immanuel Hermann von Fichte, published in 1830–1831.—Tr.

Revelation,' and of presenting it to him instead of a letter of introduction. I made a beginning with it about the thirteenth, and have since worked at it without intermission.—On the eighteenth of August I at last sent my finished work to Kant, and on the twenty-fifth paid him a visit in order to hear his opinion of it. He received me with the most marked kindness, and appeared very well satisfied with my dissertation. We did not come to any close philosophical discourse. With regard to my philosophical doubts, he referred me to his ' Critique of Pure Reason,' and to the court chaplain, Schulz, whom I shall at once find out. On the twenty-sixth I dined with Kant in the company of Professor Sommer, and I found Kant to be a very pleasant and very intellectual man. I now for the first time recognised in him traits worthy of the great intellect that has found embodiment in his writings.—

"On the twenty-seventh I brought this journal to a close, after completing the excerpts from Kant's lectures on anthropology, lent to me by Herr von S. I also make a resolution henceforth regularly to continue this journal every evening before going to bed, and to record therein everything of interest that occurs to me, but especially noting all characteristic traits and observations.—

"The twenty-eighth; evening. Yesterday I began to revise my Critique, and fell upon right good and profound ideas, which, however, made me unhappily conscious that my first treatment of the subject was exceedingly superficial. To-day I was desirous of continuing the new line of investigation, but found myself so carried away by my imagination that I have not been able to do anything all day. In my present position this is, unfortunately, not to be wondered at. I have calculated that, counting from to-day, my means of subsistence will not suffice me here for more than fourteen days. I have, it is true, already experienced the like embarrassment, but it was in my own country; and, besides, with increase of years and a more acute sense of honour, the case is always a harder one. I have formed no resolution, nor can form any. To Pastor Borowski, to whom Kant addressed me, I shall not reveal my situation: if I reveal it to any one, it will be to no other than to Kant himself.

"On the twenty-ninth I visited Borowski, in whom I found a truly good and honourable man. He made me a proposal of a situation, but it is not yet quite an assured one; and besides, it is one for which I have no great liking. At the same time, by his frankness of manner he extorted from me the admission that it was urgent for me to obtain an appointment. He advised me to see Professor W——. Work has been an impossibility for me. On the following day I did in fact call on W——, and afterwards visited the court chaplain, Schulz. The prospects held out by the former are very uncertain; still he spoke of a tutorship in Courland, which certainly nothing but the direst necessity will induce me to accept! Later, I went to the house of the court chaplain, where I was at first received by his wife. Her husband by and by appeared, but he was absorbed in mathematical circles. Afterwards, when he understood more distinctly who I was, Kant's recommendation rendered him very friendly. He has an angular Prussian countenance, but the very spirit of loyalty and good-heartedness shines through its features. I also made the acquaintance at his house of Herr Bräunlich, and of his charge, Count Dänhof, of Herr Büttner, the court chaplain's nephew, and of a young *savant* of Nürnberg, Herr Ehrhard, a youth of good and excellent parts, though wanting in manners and without knowledge of the world.

"On the first of September I formed a decided resolution, which I wished to communicate to Kant. A situation as tutor, however regretfully I might be obliged to accept it, is not to be had, and the uncertainty of my position hinders me from working with freedom of mind, and from profiting by the instructive intercourse of my friends. I must away, then, back to my own country! The small loan of which I stand in need for this purpose may perhaps be obtained through the mediation of Kant; but as I was in the act of going to him with the object of declaring my intention, courage failed me. I decided to write to him. For the evening I was invited to the house of the court chaplain, where I spent a very pleasant evening. On the second I finished my letter to Kant and despatched it."

Despite the remarkableness of this letter, I cannot bring myself to give it here. I fancy the red blood is mounting to my cheeks, and I feel as though I were relating in the presence of strangers the most shamefaced miseries of my own family. In spite of my striving after French urbanity, in spite of my philosophic cosmopolitanism, old Germany with all its Philistine sentiments, still holds its place in my bosom. Enough, I cannot transcribe this letter, and merely relate this much:—Immanuel Kant was so poor that, notwithstanding the pathetic, heart-rending tone of this letter, he could lend Johann Gottlieb Fichte no money. But the latter showed no trace of ill-humour on that account, as may be gathered from the language of his journal, from which I continue to quote:—

"I was invited to dine with Kant on the third of September. He received me with his usual cordiality, telling me, however, that he had not as yet formed any resolution as to my proposition; that he was not in a position to do so for a fortnight. What amiable frankness! For the rest, he started objections to my plans, which betrayed that he was not sufficiently acquainted with our position in Saxony. . . . During all these days I have done nothing.

I will, however, set to work again, and simply leave the rest to God. The sixth :—I was asked to visit Kant, who proposed to me the disposing of my manuscript on 'The Critique of all Revelation' to the publisher Hartung, through the intervention of Pastor Borowski. 'It is well written,' said he, when I spoke of revising it. Is this the case? And yet it is Kant that says so! For the rest, he declined the object of my first request. On the tenth I dined with Kant. Nothing said about our affair. Master of Arts Gensichen was there, and, though only general, the conversation was in part very interesting. Kant's disposition towards me remains quite unchanged. . . . The thirteenth :—I was anxious to work to-day, and yet I get nothing done. I am overcome by dejection. How will this end? How will it be with me eight days hence? My money will then be quite exhausted."

After much wandering about, after a long sojourn in Switzerland, Fichte at last finds a settled position at Jena, and from this time dates his period of splendour. Jena and Weimar, two little Saxon towns lying within short distance of each other, were then the central points of the intellectual life of Germany. At Weimar were the court and poetry ; at Jena, the university and philosophy. *There* were the greatest poets, *here* the most learned men of Germany. In the year 1794 Fichte commenced his lectures at Jena. The date is significant, and explains the spirit of his writings at this period, as well as the tribulations to which he was henceforth exposed, and to which four years later he succumbed. For in the year 1798 were raised those accusations of atheism that drew down upon him insufferable persecutions, and occasioned his departure from Jena. This, the most noteworthy event in the life of Fichte, possesses also a general significance, and we cannot pass it over in silence.

Here, too, is naturally the place to speak of Fichte's views concerning the nature of God.

In the periodical called *The Philosophical Journal*, at that time edited by himself, Fichte published an article entitled " Development of the Notion of Religion," sent to him by a certain Forberg, a schoolmaster at Saalfield. To this article Fichte added a short explanatory dissertation, under the title, " On the Ground of our Belief in a Divine Government of the World."

Both articles were suppressed by the Government of the Electorate of Saxony, under the pretext that they were tainted with atheism. Simultaneously there was despatched from Dresden a requisition to the court of Weimar enjoining upon it the serious punishment of Professor Fichte. The court of Weimar did not, it is true, permit itself to be misled by such a demand; but as Fichte on this occasion committed the gravest blunders, amongst others that of writing an " Appeal to the Public " without the sanction of official authority, the Government of Weimar, offended at this step and importuned from other quarters, had no alternative but to administer a mild reproof to the professor who had imprudently expressed his views. Fichte, however, considering himself in the right, was unwilling to submit to such reproof, and left Jena. To judge from his letters written at this time, he was especially piqued at the conduct of two persons, whose official positions lent much weight to their voice in this affair;—these two persons were His Reverence the President of the Consistorial Council, Herr von Herder, and His Excellence the Privy Councillor, Herr von Goethe; but both are sufficiently excusable. It is pathetic to read in the posthumous letters of Herder how the poor man was embarrassed by the candidates of theology, who, after studying at Jena, came before him at

Weimar to undergo examination as Protestant preachers. About Christ the Son he no longer dared to put a single question; he was glad enough to have their mere acknowledgment of the existence of the Father. As for Goethe, he expresses himself in his Memoirs, regarding this occurrence, to the following effect :—

" After Reinhold's departure from Jena, an event justly considered a great loss for the University, the appointment of successor to him was rashly, even audaciously, conferred on Fichte, who in his writings had manifested a certain grandeur, though not perhaps the requisite tact for dealing with the most important topics of morality and politics. He was a man of as strong a personality as had ever been known, and, considered in their higher aspects, there was nothing censurable in his views; but how could he maintain himself on a footing of equality with a world that he regarded as his own created possession ?

" The hours that he desired to set apart during weekdays for his public lectures being objected to, he undertook to hold on Sundays the prelections regarding which objections were raised. The lesser adverse circumstances and the greater obstacles arising from these had scarcely been smoothed down and adjusted, when the assertions of Professor Fichte concerning God and sacred things (about which he would have done better to have maintained profound silence) attracted in outside circles troublesome observation.

" Fichte had ventured in his *Philosophical Journal* to express himself about God and sacred things in a manner that seemed contradictory to the language customarily employed in dealing with such mysteries. He was called in question for it; his defence did not improve matters, for it was undertaken with passion and without any suspicion how well disposed towards him people here were,

although they knew what interpretation to put on his
ideas and language — an interpretation of his opinions
that could not indeed be explained to him in crude
words, just as little as he could be brought to understand how help might be afforded him in the kindliest
spirit. Discussion for and against, doubts and assertions,
confirmations and resolutions, surged about the university
in many-sided uncertain discourse : there was talk of
ministerial remonstrance, of nothing short of a public
reprimand which Fichte might have to expect. Thereupon, throwing aside all moderation, he considered himself justified in addressing to the ministry a violent
letter, in which, assuming the certainty of proceedings
being taken against him, he haughtily and vehemently
declared that he would never submit to such treatment;
that he preferred, without more ado, to quit the university,
in which case he would not do so alone, as several other
influential teachers were in accord with him to leave
the place.

"As a result of this step, all friendly intentions that
had been aroused on his behalf were now restrained, nay,
even paralysed. No expedient, no compromise, was now
possible, and the gentlest measure that could be adopted
was to dismiss him without delay. Then, for the first
time, after the affair was beyond remedy, Fichte perceived the turn his friends had sought to give the affair,
and he was forced to regret his precipitation, whilst we
had reason to compassionate him."

Have we not here his very self, the ministerial Goethe
with his conciliations and prudent reticences ? In reality
he censures Fichte only for having said what he thought,
and for not having said it with the customary disguises
of expression. He does not find fault with the thought,
but with the word. That deism had been annihilated in
the world of German philosophy was, as I have already

said, a secret known to every one; a secret, however, that must not be proclaimed on the housetops. Goethe was as little a deist as Fichte; for he was a pantheist. But his very position on the heights of pantheism enabled Goethe with his sharp eyes to perceive very clearly the untenableness of the Fichtean philosophy, and his gracious lips could not forbear to smile at what he saw. To the Jews (and every deist is, after all, a Jew) the doctrine of Fichte was an abomination: to the great pagan it was only a folly. The "great pagan" is, you must understand, the name bestowed on Goethe in Germany. Yet this name is not quite appropriate. The paganism of Goethe is wonderfully modernised. His vigorous heathen nature manifests itself in his clear penetrating conception of all external facts, of all forms and colours; but Christianity has endowed him also with a profounder intelligence. Christianity, in spite of his militant antipathy towards it, has initiated him into the mysteries of the spiritual world; he has drunk of the blood of Christ, and this has made him comprehend the most secret voices of nature, like Siegfried, the hero of the "Nibelungen," who understood the language of the birds the instant that his lips were moistened by a drop of the slain dragon's blood. It is a remarkable thing that Goethe's pagan nature should have been so thoroughly pervaded by our modern sentimentality, that the antique marble of his temperament should have pulsated with so much modern feeling, and that he should have sympathised as deeply with the sufferings of young Werther as with the joys of an ancient Greek god. The pantheism of Goethe differed, therefore, very widely from that of paganism. To express my ideas briefly: Goethe was the Spinoza of poetry. The whole of Goethe's poetry is animated by the same spirit that is wafted towards us from the writings of Spinoza. That Goethe paid undivided allegiance to the doctrine of Spinoza is beyond doubt. At any rate, he occupied himself with it throughout his life; in the introductory passages of his Memoirs, as in the concluding volume recently published, he has frankly acknowledged this to be the case. I cannot now recollect where I have read that Herder, losing his temper at finding Goethe perpetually engaged with Spinoza's works, once exclaimed, " If Goethe would just for once take up some other Latin book than one of Spinoza's!" But this applies not only to Goethe; quite a number of his friends, who afterwards became more or less celebrated as poets, devoted themselves at an early period of their lives to pantheism; and this doctrine assumed a practical form in German art before it attained to supremacy amongst us as a philosophic theory. Even in Fichte's time, when idealism was flourishing most sublimely in the domain of philosophy, in the region of art it was being violently destroyed, and there had already begun in Germany that celebrated revolt in art—a revolt not yet terminated— which traces its origin to the conflict of Romanticism with the ancient Classical Régime.

Our first Romanticists were, in fact, moved by a pantheistic instinct, which they did not themselves comprehend. The sentiment, which they mistook for a yearning towards the Catholic mother Church, was of deeper origin than they suspected. Their veneration and affection for the traditions of the Middle Ages, for the popular beliefs, the diablerie, the sorcery, and the witchcraft of former times, —all this was a suddenly reawakened, though uncomprehended, predilection for the pantheism of the old Germans, and, in its foully stained and spitefully mutilated form, what they really loved was the pre-christian religion of their ancestors. I must here recall what was said in the first part of this book, where I showed how Christianity absorbed the elements of the old Germanic religion,

—how, after undergoing the most outrageous transformation, these elements were preserved in the popular beliefs
of the Middle Ages in such a way that the old worship of
nature came to be regarded as mere wicked sorcery, the
old gods as odious demons, and their chaste priestesses as
profligate witches. From this point of view the aberra-
tions of our earliest Romanticists can be more leniently
judged than is usually the case. They wished to restore
the Catholicism of the Middle Ages, for they felt that in
this Catholicism there still survived many sacred recollections of their first ancestors, many splendid memorials of
their earliest national life. It was these mutilated and
defiled relics that attracted the sympathies of the Romanticists, and they detested a Protestantism and a Liberalism
whose aim was to destroy these relics and to efface the
whole Catholic past.

I shall return, however, to this subject. At present it
is sufficient merely to mention that pantheism began in
Fichte's time to force its way into German art ; that even
Catholic Romanticists unconsciously followed this tendency, and that Goethe was its foremost spokesman.
This is already apparent in his " Werther," wherein he
aspires after a beatific identification with nature. In
" Faust " he seeks to establish relationship with nature
by a method daringly direct and mystical : he conjures
the secret forces of the earth by the magic spell of the
*Höllenzwang.** But it is in his songs that Goethe's pantheism reveals itself with greatest purity and charm.
The doctrine of Spinoza has escaped from its chrysalid
mathematical form, and flutters about us as a lyric of
Goethe, Hence the wrath displayed by our orthodox
believers and pietists against Goethe's song. With their
pious bears' paws they make clumsy efforts to seize this
butterfly that constantly eludes their grasp ; so delicately

* Influence of evil spirits over men. —TR.

ethereal, so lightly winged is Goethe's song. Frenchmen can form to themselves no conception of it unless they possess a knowledge of our language. These songs of Goethe's have a coquettish charm that is indescribable: the harmonious verses entwine themselves about the heart like a tenderly loved one; the word embraces whilst the thought kisses thee.

For our part, we do not see in Goethe's conduct regarding Fichte any of those base motives indicated in even baser language by his contemporaries. They failed to comprehend the different natures of the two men. The most moderate amongst them misinterpreted Goethe's passiveness when, at a later time, Fichte was sorely pressed and persecuted. They did not correctly appreciate Goethe's situation. This giant was minister in a liliputian German state. He could never indulge in natural movements. It was said of the seated Jupiter of Phidias at Olympia that, if he were suddenly to stand erect, he would shatter the dome of the temple. This was precisely Goethe's position at Weimar; were he suddenly to have risen from his tranquil sitting posture, he would have shattered the gable ridge of the state, or, what is more probable, would have broken his head against it. And was he, then, to encounter this risk for a doctrine that was not merely erroneous, but actually ridiculous? The German Jupiter remained calmly seated, and permitted himself to be tranquilly adored and perfumed with incense.

It would lead me too far from my subject were I to seek from the standpoint of the artistic interests of this epoch more completely to justify Goethe's conduct with regard to the accusation against Fichte. In Fichte's favour there is the sole circumstance that the accusation was a mere pretext behind which political motives were concealed; for a theologian may with reason be accused of atheism, since he has accepted the obligation of teaching certain doctrines. A philosopher, however, does not and cannot enter into such an obligation, and his thought remains free as the bird of the air. It is, perhaps, unjust of me that, partly in order to spare my own, partly in order to spare the feelings of others, I have not stated here all the circumstances on which the accusation against Fichte was founded and justified. I will cite only one of the dubious passages in the incriminating treatise :—

"The living and active moral order is God himself; we need no other God, nor can we comprehend any other. There is no ground in human reason for going beyond this moral order of the universe, and for admitting, as a conclusion from effect to cause, some special being as the source of this effect. The primitive intelligence of man certainly does not confirm this conclusion, and is ignorant of such a being; only a philosophy capable of self-misapprehension can deduce it."

With characteristic obstinacy, Fichte, in his "Appeal to the Public" and in his "Judicial Vindication," reiterated his views more strongly and more glaringly, and in language, too, that wounds our deepest feelings. We, who believe in a real God, a God that reveals himself to our senses in infinite space and to our spirit in infinite thought; we, who adore in nature a visible God, and who recognise in our inmost soul his mysterious voice; we are repelled by the harsh, even ironical terms in which Fichte declares our God to be a mere chimera. It is doubtful, indeed, whether there is irony or mental extravagance in Fichte's endeavour to eliminate from the being of God all sentient attributes, and thus to deny his very existence, since existence is a sentient notion, and is only possible as such! "The theory of knowledge," he says, "knows no other mode of existence than a sentient one, and, as existence is attributable only to the phenomena of experience, this predicate cannot apply to God." Fichte's God, therefore, has no existence; he *is* not; he manifests himself only as pure action, as a sequence of events, as *ordo ordinans,* as the law of the universe.

It is thus that idealism has filtered deity through every possible abstraction, until at last no residuum is left. Henceforth, as with you, in place of a king, with us, in place of a God, law is sovereign.

But which is more absurd, a law of atheism, that is, a law without God, or a God-law, that is, a God that is only a law?

The idealism of Fichte ranks as one of the most colossal errors ever hatched in the human brain. It is more god-less and more worthy of condemnation than the coarsest materialism. What is called in France the atheism of the materialists, is, as I might easily show, an edifying and devout doctrine when compared with the consequences of Fichte's transcendental idealism. This I know: both systems are repugnant to me. Both are also anti-poetic. The French materialists have written quite as bad verses as the German transcendental idealists; but the doctrine of Fichte was in no respect dangerous to the State, and still less merited being persecuted as such. In order to be capable of being led astray by this heresy, one must have been endowed with speculative acumen in a degree to be found amongst few men. The great mass, with its thousands of thick heads, was quite impervious to this erroneous doctrine. The views of Fichte concerning God should have been attacked, therefore, by the path of reason, and not through aid of the police. The accusation of atheism in philosophy was a thing so strange in Germany, that Fichte at first really did not understand what it meant. Quite justly did he remark that the question whether a system of philosophy is atheistical or not sounds to a philosopher as extraordinary as the question whether a triangle is green or red would sound to a mathematician.

This accusation had, then, its secret motives, as Fichte soon perceived. Being of all men the most truthful, we may implicitly believe what he says in a letter to Reinhold with respect to these secret motives. As this letter, dated the 22d of May 1779, depicts the character of the entire epoch, and conveys a clear idea of all the affliction of the man, we shall here quote a portion of it :—

"Weariness and disgust determine me to adopt the resolution, whereof I have already spoken to you, of disappearing completely for a few years. From the view I took of the state of affairs, I was convinced that duty itself demanded this resolution ; for in the midst of the present ferment I shall certainly not obtain a hearing, and I should only increase the agitation ; but after a few years, when the first feelings of surprise have calmed down, I shall be able to speak with all the more emphasis. At the present moment I think differently. I ought not now to remain mute, for if I preserve silence now, I shall never again dare to speak. Since the alliance of Russia with Austria, I have long thought probable what is now become a certainty for me after recent events, and especially after the atrocious murder of the French Ambassador, an affair about which people here are jubilant, and with reference to which Schiller and Goethe exclaimed, 'Quite right ; these dogs must be slain !' I am convinced that from this time forward despotism will defend itself with the energy of despair, that it will become consistent through Paul * and Pitt, that the basis of its plan is to root out liberty of opinion, and that the Germans will not impede the attainment of this object.

"Do not fancy, for example, that the court of Weimar

* The Czar Paul I., 1796–1801.—Tr.

feared a diminution in the number of students at the university on account of my presence there; it was too well assured of the contrary; it was *obliged* to remove me in consequence of a general agreement, strongly supported by the Electorate of Saxony. Burscher of Leipzig, who was privy to these secrets, laid a wager of a considerable sum so long ago as the end of last year, that I would be exiled before the expiry of the present year. Vogt was long since won over to my enemies through Burgsdorf. The department of sciences at Dresden has made it known that no one who devotes himself to the new philosophy will receive promotion, or, if already promoted, he shall be incapable of further advancement. In the Free School at Leipzig, Rosenmüller's [10] 'Explanatory Criticisms' were held to be of a suspicious tendency. Luther's Catechism has lately been reintroduced into this school, and the teachers have been referred back to the symbolical books. This will not end here, and it will extend. . . . To sum up: Nothing is more certain than the absolute certainty that, unless the French gain a tremendous ascendancy, and unless, within a few years, they carry through important changes in Germany, or at least in a very considerable portion of it, no man that has been known during the course of his life to have thought a free thought will be able to find in Germany a resting-place. . . . There is for me, however, one thing more certain than certainty itself, namely this, that though I were presently to find somewhere a hole wherein to conceal myself, I should, in two years at furthest, be hunted out of it again, and it is a dangerous thing to run the risk of being chased from place to place: of this we have an historical example in the case of Rousseau.

"Suppose I remain quite silent and write not another line; shall I be left in peace on this condition? I do not believe it; and admitting that, as regards the courts, I might hope for this, would not the *clergy*, wherever I might turn my steps, hound on the *populace* against me, suffer me to be stoned by it, and then solicit the governments to banish me as a person that excited tumults? But ought I then to be silent? No, verily, I ought not; for I have reason for believing that, if anything of the German spirit can be saved, it can be saved through my speech, whilst by my silence philosophy will be totally and prematurely ruined. Of those of whom I do not expect that they will leave me to exist in silence, do I still less expect that they will permit me freedom of speech.

" But I shall convince them of the harmlessness of my doctrine. Dear Reinhold, how canst thou suppose these men to be well-intentioned towards me? The fairer my character is shown to be, the more innocent it appears, the blacker do these men grow, and the more aggravated does my real crime appear. I never supposed them to be persecuting me for so-called *atheism:* what they persecuted in me was the free-thinker, who begins to make himself *intelligible* (the obscurity of his style was Kant's good fortune); what they persecuted in me was the decried *democrat;* they were terrified as by a spectre at that *independence* which, as they had a dim presentiment, my philosophy awakens." *

I once more remark that this letter is not of yesterday, but bears date the 22d of May 1799. The political circumstances of that time present an even melancholy resemblance to the most recent condition of Germany; with this single point of difference, that during the former period the spirit of liberty flourished among the learned, among poets and men of letters generally, whereas nowadays this spirit finds a far more ready utterance among the

* The whole of the long paragraph that follows was struck out by the censor in the first German editions. It is restored in the later editions. —Tr

active masses, among artisans and tradespeople. During the epoch of the first revolution, whilst a leaden, altogether Teutonic somnolence weighed down the people, whilst all Germany seemed overcome by a species of brutal repose, our literary life revealed the wildest commotion and ferment. The most solitary author, living in the remotest nook of Germany, took part in this movement; possessed of no accurate knowledge of political occurrences, by a kind of secret affinity he felt their social importance and he expressed it in his writings. This phenomenon reminds me of those large sea-shells sometimes placed as ornaments on the mantel-shelf, which, however distant they may be from the sea, at once begin to murmur when the hour of flood-tide arrives and when the waves are dashing against the shore. When the revolutionary tide began to flow in Paris, that great human ocean, when its waves surged and roared amongst you here, German hearts across the Rhine were resounding and murmuring in response. . . . But they were so isolated, surrounded as they were by mere unfeeling pieces of porcelain, tea-cups and coffee-pots and Chinese pagods, that nodded their heads mechanically as though they understood what the talk was about! Alas! our poor German predecessors had to atone most bitterly for their revolutionary sympathy. Petty nobles and canting priests played on them the coarsest and basest of their spiteful tricks. Some of them fled to Paris, and have disappeared or died here in poverty and misery. I lately saw an old blind compatriot who has remained in Paris since that time. I saw him at the Palais-Royal, whither he had come to warm himself a little in the sun. It was pitiful to behold how pale and thin he was, and how he groped his way along the sides of the houses. They told me he was the old Danish poet Heiberg.[11] I also saw not long since the garret in which citizen George Forster [12] died. But it would have fared even worse with the

friends of liberty who remained in Germany had not
Napoleon and the French made haste to conquer us.
Napoleon certainly never fancied that he had himself
been the saviour of ideology. Without his aid our philosophers, and with them their ideas, would have been
exterminated by the gibbet and the wheel. But the
German friends of liberty, too republican in their sentiments to do homage to Napoleon, and too magnanimous
to ally themselves with a foreign domination, wrapped
their thoughts in profound silence. They went about
sorrowfully with broken hearts and sealed lips. When
Napoleon fell they were seen to smile, though it was a
mournful smile, and they still remained silent. They
took scarcely the slightest interest in the patriotic enthusiasm which, with the sanction of the supreme powers,
then broke forth jubilantly throughout Germany. They
knew what they knew, and were silent. As these Republicans lead a very chaste and simple life, they usually
attain a great age, and when the Revolution of July took
place, many of them were still alive. We were not a
little astonished then at beholding the old fellows, whom
we had always been accustomed to see going about bowed
down and in almost imbecile silence, suddenly raise their
heads and smile amicably at us youngsters, and seize each
other's hands, and begin to tell merry tales. I even heard
one of them singing; for he sang to us in a café the
Marseillaise Hymn, and we learnt the melody and the
beautiful words, and it was not long till we sang it better
than the old man himself; for in the middle of the best
stanzas he would often laugh like a fool or weep like a
child. It is always a fortunate thing when such old
people remain alive to teach young ones songs. We
young ones shall not forget these songs, and some of us
will one day teach them by heart to grandchildren yet
unborn; but many of us will have rotted by that time,

some in the prisons of home, some in the garrets of exile.

Let us speak of philosophy again ! I have shown how the philosophy of Fichte, though constructed of the most attenuated abstractions, presented a rigid inflexibility in its consequences, which were pursued to the most audacious extremes. But one fine morning we perceived a great change in this philosophy ; it began to blossom with innocent flowers and to weep childishly; it became tender and modest. The Titan of idealism, who had climbed up to heaven by the ladder of thought, and had groped about with daring hand in its empty chambers, now becomes a creature bowed down with Christian humility, who sighs much about love. This is Fichte's second period, and concerns us little here. His entire system of philosophy undergoes the strangest modifications. About this time he wrote a book, lately translated into French, "The Destiny of Man." A book of a similar character, "Instruction towards Attaining the Celestial Life," also belongs to this period.

Fichte, the opinionative man, would, of course, never admit this great transformation. He maintained that his philosophy was always the same, that it was merely its mode of expression that had undergone change and improvement; people had never understood him. He contended, too, that the *Philosophy of Nature*, which had sprung up in Germany and which was supplanting idealism, was in principle precisely the same as his own system, and that his pupil, Herr Joseph Schelling, in detaching himself from his master and in introducing this new philosophy, had merely remodelled the nomenclature of the old philosophy, and had merely amplified his old doctrine by the addition of barren accessories.

This brings us to a new phase of German thought. We have just mentioned the names *Joseph Schelling* and

Philosophy of Nature; but as the former is almost quite unknown in France, and as the expression *Philosophy of Nature* is not very generally understood, I must explain the significance of both names. It will certainly not be possible to do so exhaustively in this sketch; at present we shall only utter a warning against certain insidious errors, and merely draw attention to the social importance of this philosophy.

At the outset it may be said that Fichte was not very far wrong in contending that Herr Joseph Schelling's doctrine was in reality his own merely amplified and formulated in different terms. Precisely like Herr Joseph Schelling does Fichte teach:—there exists but one being, the *Ego*, the absolute; he also teaches the identity of the ideal and the real. In the "Theory of Philosophy," as already shown, Fichte sought by means of an intellectual act to construct the real out of the ideal. Joseph Schelling, however, has reversed the process; he endeavours to explain the ideal by the real. To express my meaning more clearly: Starting from the axiom that thought and nature are one, Fichte, by an operation of the intellect, arrives at the external world; by thought he creates nature, by the ideal the real. For Schelling, on the contrary, though he starts from the same axiom, the external world resolves itself into pure ideas; nature for him becomes thought, the real becomes ideal. Each of these tendencies, that of Fichte and that of Schelling, is to a certain extent the complement of the other. For, accepting as ultimate the axiom just referred to, philosophy naturally falls into two parts, in one of which it would be shown how from the idea nature rises to phenomenal reality; in the other, how nature resolves itself into pure ideas. Philosophy may therefore be divided into *Transcendental Idealism* and into *Philosophy of Nature.* Now both of these sides were really acknowledged by Schelling: the latter he followed out in his "Ideas towards a Philosophy of Nature," the former in his "System of Transcendental Idealism."

I refer to these works (of which one appeared in 1797, the other in 1800) merely because those two reciprocally complementary sides are expressed in their very titles, and not because they contain a complete system. No; such a system is to be found in none of Schelling's works. He, unlike Kant and Fichte, has no chief work that may be regarded as the central point of his philosophy. It would be an injustice to judge Schelling by the contents of a book, and by a rigorous interpretation of the letter. One should rather read his works in chronological order, follow up the gradual development of his thought, and then take firm grasp of his fundamental idea. Indeed, it seems to me often necessary, in reading his works, to distinguish where thought ceases and where poetry begins; for Schelling is one of those beings endowed by nature with more poetic temperament than poetic power—one who, incapable of satisfying the daughters of Parnassus, has fled to the woodlands of philosophy, where he has contracted with abstract hamadryads a barren union. The sentiment of such natures is poetic, but the instrument, the word, is feeble; they strive in vain after an artistic form wherein to communicate their thoughts and their knowledge. Poetry is at once Schelling's strength and his weakness. It is here that he is distinguished from Fichte as much to his advantage as to his disadvantage. Fichte is merely a philosopher; his power consists in his dialectic, and his strength in ability to demonstrate. This, however, is Schelling's weak side; he lives in a world of intuition; he does not feel at home on the cold heights of logic; he stretches forth eager hands towards the flowery valleys of symbolism, and his philosophical strength lies in the art of construction. But this is an intellectual aptitude found as frequently amongst mediocre poets as amongst the best philosophers.

From this last indication it becomes clear that Schelling, in so much of his philosophy as is pure transcendental idealism, remained, and could not but remain, a mere echoer of Fichte; whilst in the philosophy of nature, where he has to deal with flowers and stars, he cannot help blossoming and shining radiantly. Not only he himself, but also like-minded friends attached themselves by preference to this side of his philosophy, and the commotion thereby aroused was only a kind of reaction of poetasters against the former abstract philosophy of the intellect. Like school-children freed from their tasks after sighing all day in close rooms under the burden of syntax and arithmetic, the scholars of Schelling rushed out of doors to nature, to the fragrant sunny world of the real, and huzzaed and turned summersaults and made a great disturbance.

The expression "scholars of Schelling" must certainly not be taken in its customary sense. Schelling himself tells us it was only a school such as existed among the ancient poets that he desired to found, a school of poetry in which no one was bound to accept a particular doctrine or to submit to a special discipline, but one in which each was to obey the idea, and to manifest it in his own manner. He might also have said that he wished to found a school of prophets, where the inspired should begin to prophesy as fancy moved them, and in whatever dialect they pleased. This, indeed, was done by those disciples whom the master's spirit had deeply moved; the most shallow-brained began to prophesy each in a different tongue, and philosophy had its great day of Pentecost.

Things gravest and most sublime may be turned into masquerade and buffoonery; a rabble of cowardly knaves and melancholy clowns is capable of compromising a great idea: this we see in the case of the philosophy of nature. But the ridicule brought upon this philosophy by Schelling's school of the prophets or school of the poets ought not really to be imputed to it, for the idea on which the philosophy of nature rests is indeed nothing else than the idea of Spinoza, than pantheism.

The doctrine of Spinoza and the philosophy of nature, as explained by Schelling during his best period, are essentially one and the same thing. The Germans having reached the stage of despising the materialism of Locke, and having pursued to its last consequences the idealism of Leibnitz and found it equally unfruitful, arrived finally at the third son of Descartes—at Spinoza. Philosophy had once more described a great circle, the same, it may be said, that it had already traversed two thousand years before in Greece. But a closer comparison of these two circuits of human thought reveals an essential difference. Amongst the Greeks there were as daring sceptics as amongst ourselves; the Eleatics were as decided in their denial of the reality of the external world as our modern transcendental idealists. Plato rediscovered the world of thought in the phenomenal world as plainly as did Schelling. But we had this advantage over the Greeks as well as over the Cartesian school: we commenced our philosophic circuit by an investigation of the sources of human knowledge, by the "Critique of Pure Reason" of our Immanuel Kant.

The mention of Kant affords me an opportunity of adding to the foregoing observations, that one species of evidence in favour of the existence of God, the so-called moral evidence, with which Kant did not interfere, was overthrown with great *éclat* by Schelling. I have already remarked, however, that this evidence was not very conclusive, and that Kant perhaps allowed it to subsist from promptings of good-nature. The God of Schelling is the

God-universe of Spinoza—at least he was so in the year 1801, in the second volume of the *Journal of Speculative Physics.* Here God is the absolute identity of nature and thought, of matter and mind; and absolute identity is not the cause of the universe, but is the universe itself, consequently the God-universe. In it there exist neither opposites nor divisions. Absolute identity is also absolute totality. A year later Schelling still further developed his God in a work entitled, " Bruno; or, Concerning the Divine and Natural Principles of Things." This title recalls the most noble martyr of our doctrine, Giordano Bruno of Nola, of glorious memory. The Italians asserted that Schelling borrowed all his best ideas from old Bruno, and they accused him of plagiarism. They were wrong, for there is no such thing as plagiarism in philosophy. In the year 1804 the God of Schelling appeared at last in His complete form in a work entitled " Philosophy and Religion." It is here that we have in its completed form the theory of the absolute expressed in three formulas. The first of these is the categorical: The absolute is neither the ideal nor the real (neither mind nor matter), but is the identity of both. The second formula is the hypothetical: When subject and object are present, the absolute is the essential equality of both. The third formula is the disjunctive: There is only *one* being, but this unity of being may be regarded at one and the same time, or by turns, as wholly ideal or as wholly real. The first formula is strictly negative; the second supposes a condition more difficult to comprehend than the hypothesis itself; and the third formula is exactly that of Spinoza: absolute substance is cognisable either as thought or as extension. Along the path of philosophy, then, Schelling could proceed no further than Spinoza, since the absolute can be comprehended only under the form of these two attributes, thought and extension. But at this point Schelling leaves the philosophical route, and seeks by a kind of mystical intuition to arrive at the contemplation of the absolute itself; he seeks to contemplate it in its central point, in its essence, where it is neither ideal nor real, neither thought nor extension, neither subject nor object, neither mind nor matter, but . . . I know not what!

Here philosophy ceases with Schelling, and poetry—I may say folly—commences. But it is here that he meets with the greatest sympathy from a number of silly admirers whom it suits admirably to abandon calm reflection, and who, as if in imitation of the dancing dervishes described by our friend Jules David, continue spinning round in a circle until objective and subjective worlds become lost to them,—until both worlds melt into a colourless nothingness, that is neither real nor ideal, until they see things invisible, hear what is inaudible, until they hear colours and see tones, until the absolute reveals itself to them.

I am of opinion that with this attempt intellectually to conceive the absolute Schelling's philosophic career comes to a close. A greater thinker now steps on the scene, one who rounds into a completed system the philosophy of nature, explains from this synthesis the whole world of phenomena, supplements the great ideas of his predecessors by yet greater ideas, subjects their philosophy to every form of discipline, and thus establishes it on a scientific basis. He is the scholar of Schelling, a scholar, however, who, making himself by degrees possessor of all his master's might in the realm of philosophy, outgrows his master, and finally thrusts him into obscurity. This is the great Hegel, greatest of philosophers begotten by Germany since Leibnitz. There can be no doubt that he far overtops Kant and Fichte. To the penetration of the former and to the vigour of the latter he adds the tranquillity of a mind that works by constitutional methods, a

harmony of thought not to be found in either Kant or
Fichte, in both of whom the revolutionary spirit is pre-
dominant. No comparison is possible between this man
and Joseph Schelling; for Hegel was a man of character.
And though, like Schelling, he may have given support
by certain suspicious vindications to the existing order of
affairs in church and state, he did so in favour of a state
that, in theory at least, rendered homage to the principle
of progress, and in favour of a church that regarded the
principle of unrestrained inquiry as its vital element; and
he made no secret of this ; he avowed all his intentions.
Schelling, on the contrary, goes cringing about in the
ante-chambers of practical and theoretical absolutism, in
the dens of Jesuitism he lends a hand in forging intellectual manacles, and all the while he tries to make believe
he is still the same unperverted child of light that he
once was ; he apostatises his apostasy, and to the shame
of deserting his cause he adds the cowardice of lying!

We may not disguise it, either from motives of piety or
of prudence; we will make no secret of it; the man who
was once the boldest exponent in Germany of the religion
of pantheism, he who proclaimed most loudly the sanctification of nature and the redintegration of man in his
divine rights, has become apostate to his own doctrine;
he has forsaken the altar consecrated by his own hands;
he has slunk back to the religious kennels of the past; he
is now a good Catholic, and preaches an extra-mundane
personal God, " who has committed the folly of creating
the world." The followers of the old orthodoxy may, if
they choose, ring their church-bells and sing " Kyrie
Eleison " over such a conversion; it proves nothing, however, in favour of their doctrine; it merely proves that man
turns to religion for support when he grows old and weary,
when his physical and intellectual powers fail him, when
he can no longer either enjoy or reason. So many free-

thinkers, you say, have been converted on their deathbed! But, at any rate, do not boast of this! Such stories belong at best to pathology, and are very bad evidence for your case. After all, they only prove that it was impossible for you to convert these free-thinkers so long as they went about under God's free sky in the enjoyment of their healthy senses and in full possession of their reasoning faculty.

It is Ballanche, I think, who says, that it is a law of nature that initiators die as soon as they have completed the work of initiation. Alas! worthy Ballanche, that is only part of the truth, and I might with more reason assert that, when the work of initiation is complete, the initiator dies—or becomes apostate. And so we may, perhaps, mitigate to a certain extent the severe judgment pronounced by intelligent Germany on Herr Schelling; we may, perhaps, commute the heavy sentence of contempt under which he lies into silent commiseration; and his desertion of his own doctrine we may explain as a consequence of the natural law in accordance with which, whenever any one has devoted all his energies to the expression or to the carrying out of an idea and has accomplished his task, that person falls exhausted, either into the arms of death, or into the embrace of his former opponents.

Such an explanation as the foregoing may enable us to understand certain other more terrible phenomena of our day which deeply afflict us. It may enable us to comprehend why men who have sacrificed everything for their opinion, who have fought and suffered for that opinion, should, after the victory is gained, abandon it and pass over into the enemy's camp! I may be permitted also, after such an explanation, to draw attention to the fact that not Joseph Schelling only, but, in some sort, both Kant and Fichte, may likewise be accused of defection.

Fichte died opportunely enough before his desertion of his own philosophy had time to become very notorious; but Kant is unfaithful to the "Critique of Pure Reason," even whilst writing the "Critique of Practical Reason." The initiator dies or becomes apostate!

I know not how it comes that this last sentence affects my soul with such a melancholy influence that I do not feel sufficient strength here to record the other bitter truths regarding the present Herr Schelling. Let us rather say something in praise of that dear former Schelling, whose memory blossoms perennially in the annals of German thought; for the former Schelling, like Kant and Fichte, represents one of the great phases of our philosophical revolution, compared by me in these pages to the political revolution in France. In truth, while in Kant we see the terrorist Convention, and in Fichte the Napoleonic Empire, in Schelling we behold the reaction of the Restoration which followed the Empire. But it was at first a restoration in a better sense. Schelling re-established nature in its legitimate rights; he aimed at a reconciliation between mind and nature; he sought to reunite them in the eternal soul of the world. He restored that great philosophy of nature which we find in the old Greek philosophers, which Socrates first drew into closer relation with the human spirit, and which thereafter flowed forth again as the ideal. He restored that great philosophy of nature which, after unobtrusively budding out of the old pantheistic religion of the Germans, displayed during the age of Paracelsus its fairest flowers, but was stifled by the introduction of Cartesianism. Alas! he ended by restoring things whereby he may in the worst sense be compared with the French Restoration. But public reason did not long endure such things; he was ignominiously driven from the throne of thought. Hegel, his major-domo, carried off his crown and shaved his head, and since then the deposed Schelling has lived as a poor shaveling in Munich, a city that preserves in its very name its monkish character, and in Latin is called *Monacho monachorum.* There I saw him, with his large pale eyes and depressed, stupefied countenance, moving about irresolutely like a spectre, a miserable picture of fallen royalty. Hegel, however, had himself crowned at Berlin, unfortunately with some slight ceremony of anointing, and he has ever since held sway over German philosophy.

Our philosophical revolution is concluded; Hegel has closed its great circle. Henceforth we see only the developing and perfecting of the philosophy of nature. This philosophy has, as I have already said, forced its way into all sciences, and has produced the most extraordinary and the most grandiose results. Much that is distressing, as I have also indicated, has of necessity come to light. These phenomena are so numerous that the mere record of them would fill an entire book. This is the really interesting and richly coloured part of our philosophical history. I am convinced, however, that it will be more profitable for Frenchmen to know nothing about it, for knowledge of this sort could only tend to produce greater confusion in French intellects; many of the propositions of the philosophy of nature, if detached from their connection, might cause much mischief amongst you. Of this at least I am certain, had you been acquainted in the year 1830 with the German philosophy of nature, you could not have produced the Revolution of July. There was necessary for the accomplishment of this act a concentration of ideas and of forces, a generous partiality, a certain virtue, a self-sufficing absence of reflection such as only your old school of philosophy rendered possible. Perverse philosophical ideas, which might in case of need have served to justify legitimacy and the doctrine of the incarnation, would have damped your enthusiasm, would have paralysed your courage. I regard it therefore as an important fact in the history of the world that your great eclectic,* who at that epoch was desirous of giving you instruction in German philosophy, had not the slightest comprehension of the subject. His providential ignorance was salutary for France and for the whole of humanity.

Alas! the philosophy of nature, which in many regions of knowledge, especially in the natural sciences strictly so called, produced the most splendid fruits, would elsewhere have brought forth the most obnoxious weeds. Whilst Oken, one of the most highly gifted thinkers, and one of the greatest citizens of Germany, was discovering his new worlds of ideas, and was inspiring the youth of Germany with enthusiasm for the imprescriptible rights of humanity, for freedom and equality,—alas! at that very time Adam Müller was lecturing on the stall-feeding of nations according to the principles of natural philosophy; at that very time Herr Görres was preaching the obscurantism of the Middle Ages from the physical science point of view, and was declaring the state to be only a tree which ought also to have in its organic distribution a stem, branches, and leaves, all as may be beautifully seen in the hierarchic corporations of the Middle Ages; at that very time Herr Steffens was proclaiming the law of philosophy in virtue of which the peasantry is distinguished from the nobility, the peasant being by nature destined to labour without enjoying, whereas the noble is entitled to enjoy without labouring; yea, only a few months since, as I am told, a dolt of a country squire in Westphalia, an arrant blockhead, bearing, I believe, the cognomen Haxthausen, published a pamphlet wherein he solicited the Government of the King of Prussia to have regard to the consistent parallel demonstrated by philosophy as existing in the organisation of the world, and to mark more strictly political distinc-

* Victor Cousin.—[Tr.]

tions; for as in nature there are four elements, fire, air, earth, and water, so in society there are four analogous elements, the nobility, the clergy, the burgesses, and the peasants.

When such melancholy follies were seen to spring from the tree of philosophy and to expand into poisonous flowers, when in particular it was observed that young Germany, absorbed in metaphysical abstractions, was oblivious to the most urgent questions of the time and had become unfit for practical life, well might patriots and friends of liberty feel a righteous indignation against philosophy, whilst some of them went the length of utterly condemning it as a vain and profitless pursuit of shadows.[13]

We shall not commit the folly of seriously confuting these malcontents. German philosophy is an important fact; it concerns the whole human race, and only our latest descendants will be in a position to decide whether we are to be praised or blamed for having first worked out our philosophy and afterwards our revolution. It seems to me that a methodical people, such as we are, must begin with the reformation, must then occupy itself with systems of philosophy, and that only after their completion could it pass to the political revolution. I find this sequence quite rational. The heads that have first served for the speculations of philosophy can afterwards be struck off by the revolution for whatever object it pleases; but philosophy would not have been able to utilise the heads struck off by a revolution that preceded it. Give yourselves no anxiety however, ye German Republicans; the German revolution will not prove any milder or gentler because it was preceded by the "Critique" of Kant, by the "Transcendental Idealism" of Fichte, or even by the Philosophy of Nature. These doctrines served to develop revolutionary forces that only await their time to break forth and to fill the world with terror and with admiration. Then will appear Kantians as little tolerant of piety in the world of deeds as in the world of ideas, who will mercilessly upturn with sword and axe the soil of our European life in order to extirpate the last remnants of the past. There will come upon the scene armed Fichteans whose fanaticism of will is to be restrained neither by fear nor by self-interest; for they live in the spirit; they defy matter like those early Christians who could be subdued neither by bodily torments nor by bodily delights. Yea, in a time of social revolution these transcendental idealists will prove even more pertinacious than the early Christians; for the latter endured earthly martyrdom in the hope of attaining celestial blessedness, whilst the transcendental idealist looks on martyrdom itself as a vain show, and is invulnerable within the intrenchment of his own thought. But most of all to be feared would be the philosophers of nature were they actively to mingle in a German revolution, and to identify themselves with the work of destruction. For if the hand of the Kantian strikes with strong unerring blow, his heart being stirred by no feeling of traditional awe; if the Fichtean courageously defies every danger, since for him danger has in reality no existence;—the Philosopher of Nature will be terrible in this, that he has allied himself with the primitive powers of nature, that he can conjure up the demoniac forces of old German pantheism; and having done so, there is aroused in him that ancient German eagerness for battle which combats not for the sake of destroying, not even for the sake of victory, but merely for the sake of the combat itself. Christianity—and this is its fairest merit —subdued to a certain extent the brutal warrior ardour of the Germans, but it could not entirely quench it; and when the cross, that restraining talisman, falls to pieces, then will break forth again the ferocity of the old combatants, the frantic Berserker rage whereof Northern poets have said and sung so much. The talisman has become rotten, and the day will come when it will pitifully crumble to dust. The old stone gods will then arise from the forgotten ruins and wipe from their eyes the dust of centuries, and Thor with his giant hammer will arise again, and he will shatter the Gothic cathedrals. . . . When ye hear the trampling of feet and the clashing of arms, ye neighbours' children, ye French, be on your guard, and see that ye mingle not in the fray going on amongst us at home in Germany. It might fare ill with you. See that ye take no hand in kindling the fire ; see that ye attempt not to extinguish it. You might easily burn your fingers in the flame. Smile not at my counsel, at the counsel of a dreamer, who warns you against Kantians, Fichteans, Philosophers of Nature. Smile not at the fantasy of one who foresees in the region of reality the same outburst of revolution that has taken place in the region of intellect. The thought precedes the deed as the lightning the thunder. German thunder is of true German character : it is not very nimble, but rumbles along somewhat slowly. But come it will, and when ye hear a crashing such as never before has been heard in the world's history, then know that at last the German thunderbolt has fallen. At this commotion the eagles will drop dead from the skies and the lions in the farthest wastes of Africa will bite their tails and creep into their royal lairs. There will be played in Germany a drama compared to which the French Revolution will seem but an innocent idyl. At present, it is true, everything is tolerably quiet; and though here and there some few men create a little stir, do not imagine these are to be the real actors in the piece. They are only little curs chasing one another round the empty arena, barking and snapping at one another, till the appointed hour when the troop of gladiators appear to fight for life and death.

And the hour will come. As on the steps of an amphitheatre, the nations will group themselves around Germany to witness the terrible combat. I counsel you, ye French, keep very quiet, and, above all, see that ye do not applaud. We might readily misunderstand such applause, and, in our rude fashion, somewhat roughly put you to silence. For, if formerly in our servile, listless mood we could oftentimes overpower you, much easier were it for us to do so in the arrogance of our new-born enthusiasm for liberty. Ye yourselves know what, in such a case, men can do; and ye are no longer in such a case. Take heed, then! I mean it well with you; therefore it is I tell you the bitter truth. Ye have more to fear from a free Germany than from the entire Holy Alliance with all its Croats and Cossacks. For, in the first place, they do not love you in Germany, which is almost incomprehensible, since ye are so amiable, and during your stay amongst us took such pains to please at least the better and fairer half of the German people. But even though this half still loved you, it is precisely the half that does not bear arms, and whose friendship, therefore, would be of little help to you. What you are really accused of I could never understand. Once in a beer-cellar at Göttingen I heard a young Old-German assert that it was necessary to be revenged on France for Conradin of Hohenstaufen, whom you beheaded at Naples. Doubtless ye have long since forgotten that: we, however, forget nothing. Ye see, then, that whenever we have a mind to quarrel with you there will be no lack of valid grounds. In any case, I advise you to be on your guard. Happen what may in Germany, though the Crown Prince of Prussia or Dr. Wirth should attain supremacy, be ye ever armed; remain quietly at your post, your weapons in your hands.   I mean it well with you, and I was seized with dismay when I heard it said lately that your Ministry proposed to disarm France.

As ye are, despite your present romantic tendency, a born classical people, ye know Olympus.   Amongst the joyous gods and goddesses quaffing and feasting of nectar and ambrosia, ye may behold one goddess, who, amidst such gaiety and pastime, wears ever a coat of mail, the helm on her head and the spear in her hand.

She is the goddess of Wisdom.

APPENDIX.

APPENDIX.

———◆———

IN translating these introductory paragraphs, the latest edition of the French version has been followed. In the *Revue des Deux Mondes* a single short paragraph stood in place of the amplified and more explicit statement in the later editions. In the German version, again, the corresponding paragraphs vary from the text of the French version. The book is introduced to German readers in the following manner :—

" Frenchmen have lately been in the habit of supposing that an acquaintance with the productions of our polite literature is sufficient to enable them to comprehend Germany. Such an acquaintance, however, has only served to raise them from a condition of total ignorance to a condition of superficial knowledge ; for the productions of our literature remain for them mere dead flowers, and the whole circle of German thought presents but a dreary enigma to them so long as they do no not understand the significance of Religion and Philosophy in Germany.

" In endeavouring to elucidate to a certain extent these two subjects, I believe that I am undertaking a useful work. For me it is no light task. It is of primary importance to avoid the technicalities of a scholastic language with which Frenchmen are totally unacquainted.

Besides, I have not studied deeply enough the subtilties either of theology or of metaphysics to be in a position to formulate them in a manner sufficiently simple and brief to meet the requirements of the French public. I shall therefore deal only with the great questions that are discussed in German divinity and philosophy; I shall attempt to illustrate merely their social importance, and throughout this book I shall keep clearly in view the limited nature of my own resources as an expositor, and the capacity of French readers for comprehending the subject.

" Great German philosophers who may happen to glance at these pages will haughtily shrug their shoulders at the inadequate treatment of whatever is here presented. May I beg them, however, kindly to bear in mind that the little I have to say will be quite clearly and intelligibly expressed ; whereas their works, though doubtless very erudite, vastly erudite, very profound, stupidly profound, are likewise as incomprehensible as they are profound. What do locked granaries profit the people so long as it has no key wherewith to open them ? The people hungers for bread, and is ready to thank me for the morsel of intellectual food which I honestly share with them.

" I do not believe that it is want of talent that restrains most of our German men of learning from giving popular expression to their views on religion and philosophy. I believe that it is dread of the consequences of their own intellectual research that prevents them communicating its results to the people. I, however, do not possess this dread, for I am no man of learning; I am myself of the people. I am no learned man, I am not among the number of the seven hundred wise men of Germany. I am one of the great crowd standing before the gates of their wisdom, and should any truth chance to slip through and find its way to me, then it has come far enough : I write it down on paper in fair characters, and give it to the compositor; he sets it up in leaden type and passes it to the printer, who prints it, and then it belongs to the whole world.

"The religion in which we in Germany rejoice is Christianity. It will be my duty then to explain what Christianity is, how it became Roman Catholicism, how from this it became Protestantism, and how German philosophy is the offspring of Protestantism.

"In beginning with the discussion of religion I premonish all pious souls not on any account to entertain the slightest anxiety.

"Fear not, pious souls!" &c.

---

[2] *Page* 25.

A short paragraph is here omitted in the latest French edition. Its omission is no doubt due to the fact that Heine's views about democracy underwent considerable change between the date when he wrote and the date when he last revised his book.

"It is, perhaps, because the great ones of this earth are certain of their supremacy, and because they are at heart resolved to go on for ever abusing this supremacy by turning it to our misfortune, that they are convinced of the necessity of Christianity for their peoples; and it is in reality a tender impulse of benevolence that prompts them to take so much trouble in upholding this religion!"

The succeeding paragraph begins with the words—"The ultimate fate of Christianity depends, then, on whether we still have need of it," altered in the latest French edition to : "The duration of religions," &c., as at page 25.

---

[3] *Page* 41.

This paragraph reads as follows in the German version :—

" I have already frequently made use of the words *spiritualism* and *sensualism*. These words, however, have here no reference, such as they have when employed by French philosophers, to the two different sources of our knowledge : I employ them, as may be gathered from the general drift of the foregoing remarks, to designate those two different modes of thought, of which one mode desires, by the destruction of matter, to glorify the spirit, whilst the other mode seeks to vindicate the natural rights of matter against the usurpations of the spirit."

[4] *Page* 41.

Instead of these opening sentences this paragraph in the latest German edition begins thus :—

" To the above-mentioned beginnings of the Lutheran Reformation—beginnings which already revealed the whole spirit of that event—I must draw special attention, since there are still current here in France regarding the Reformation the old misconceptions which were spread abroad by Bossuet through his ' Histoire des Variations,' and which are even repeated by modern writers."

[5] *Page* 58.

Luther's Hymn has found several English translators, Thomas Carlyle being the earliest of them. Catherine Winkworth's translation—probably the one best known—is to be found in her " Christian Singers of Germany," and in various collections of hymns. The present rendering is a very halting attempt to preserve the form as well as the spirit of the original. Readers of German will at once perceive how greatly superior would be a translation that accurately reproduced the rugged metre without sacrificing the fervour and vigour of the "mail-clad words" to a merely rhythmical version, however skilfully achieved. But the former task would be far more difficult of accomplishment than the latter.

----

[6] *Page 58.*

At this point the first part of the French version closes, but in the German version Heine goes on to draw a comparison between modern and early German literature. This comparison is made to turn chiefly on the distinction between the "Classical" and the "Romantic" treatment of the subject-matter in literature. A more general and more inclusive definition of these much-abused terms is given by Heine in his "Romantic School." For the sake of completeness, however, a translation of what follows in the German version is here given.

["In order to show that modern German literature begins with Luther and not with Hans Sachs], it is sufficient to indicate clearly the contrast between our new and our older literatures.

"In surveying German literature as it flourished before Luther's time, we arrive at the following conclusions:—

"1. Its material, its subject-matter, like the life itself of the Middle Ages, consists of a mingling of two heterogeneous elements, which during a long period struggled with each other in such close contact that at last they became blended together: these two elements were Germanic nationality and Indo-Gnostic, so-called Catholic Christianity.

" 2. The treatment of the subject-matter, or rather the
spirit in which it was treated, in this older literature, was
Romantic. The term 'Romantic' is erroneously applied
also to the material of that literature, as it is to all
manifestations of the Middle Ages that spring from the
blending of the two elements referred to — Germanic
nationality and Catholic Christianity. For as certain
poets of the Middle Ages treated Greek history and
mythology in a spirit truly Romantic, so Mediæval
customs and legends may be represented in a classical
form. The terms 'Classic' and 'Romantic' refer, therefore, merely to the spirit of the treatment. The treatment is Classic when the form of the representation is
identical with the idea to be represented, as is the case
in Greek works of art in which the closest harmony
exists between form and idea. The treatment is Romantic
when the form does not reveal the idea through identity
with it, but leaves the idea to be conjectured parabolically. I here use the word 'parabolically' in preference
to the word 'symbolically.' Greek mythology possessed
an array of deities, each of whom, besides identity of form
and idea, might acquire a symbolic signification. But in
this Greek religion it was only the outward fashion of
the divinities that presented anything definite,—all else,
their life and conduct, was left to the voluntary caprice
of the poet. In the Christian religion, on the other hand,
there are no such definite personalities,—there are only
definite facts, definite sacred events and actions into
which the creative faculty of man might import a parabolic significance. It has been said that Homer invented
the Greek gods; this is not true: they already existed
in definite outlines; what Homer did was to invent
their history. Artists of the Middle Ages, on the other
hand, never dared to invent the slightest detail in the
historical part of their religion:—the fall of man, the

incarnation, the baptism, the crucifixion, and so forth, were indisputable facts which could not be moulded anew, but to which the creative genius of man might impart a parabolic signification. In this parabolic spirit all the arts of the Middle Ages worked, and their treatment is Romantic. Hence the mystical universalism of the poetry of the Middle Ages; the figures are shadowy, all their actions are indefinite, everything about them has a twilight aspect as if illuminated by uncertain moonlight; the idea is signified in the form only as an enigma, and we see merely vague forms such as were appropriate to a spiritualistic literature. There is not, as with the Greeks, a sunbright harmony between form and idea; but oftentimes the idea towers above the given form to which the latter strives despairingly to attain, and thus we have a fantastic and strange sublimity; oftentimes the form quite overtops the idea when some foolish paltry thought drags itself along encumbered by a colossal form, and then we have a grotesque farce; almost always do we find deformity.

" 3. It was a universal characteristic of the older literature of which we speak that in all its productions it manifested the firm and settled faith that dominated all things temporal as well as spiritual during its epoch. Every opinion of the time was based on authorities; the poet trod with the surefootedness of a mule paths that lay among the precipices of doubt, and his works are pervaded by a daring calm, by a holy confidence that became impossible in a later age when the highest authority—the authority of the pope—was overthrown, and when all other authorities toppled down after it. All the poetry of the Middle Ages possesses the same character; it seems as though it had not been composed by individual men, but by the whole people; it is objective, epic, naïf.

" But in the literature that burst into blossom under the

influence of Luther we find quite the opposite of all this.

" 1. Its material, the subject-matter with which it has to deal, is the conflict between the interests and opinions of the Reformation and the old order of things. To the new spirit of the age the mongrel creed springing from the two elements referred to—German nationality and Indo-Gnostic Christianity—is utterly repugnant. The latter element it regards as heathen idolatry, which must give place to the true religion of the Judaic-Deistic gospel. A new order of things takes shape, the spirit makes discoveries that promote the well-being of matter; by the development of industrial pursuits and by philosophy spiritualism becomes discredited in public opinion; the third estate emerges; the roar of the revolution begins to echo in human hearts and heads; and what the age feels and thinks, what it needs and will have, it gives expression to, and this is the material of modern literature.

" 2. The spirit of treatment is no longer Romantic, but Classic. Through the revival of ancient literature a joyous enthusiasm for Greek and Latin authors diffused itself over all Europe, and men of learning, the only men who in those days wrote, strove to possess themselves of the spirit of classical antiquity, or at any rate sought in their writings to imitate classical forms of art. If, unlike the Greeks, they failed to attain harmony of form and idea, all the more strictly did they hold to the externals of Greek treatment: they distinguished, according to Greek precept, the species of form; they refrained from all Romantic extravagance; and in this respect we call them classical.

" 3. The universal characteristic of modern literature is the predominance in it of individuality and of scepticism. The authorities are dethroned; reason is now the only lamp to illumine the steps of man; conscience his only guiding-staff in the dark labyrinth of this life. Man now stands face to face alone with his creator and sings to him his lay. Thus our modern literature begins with spiritual songs. Later on, however, as literature becomes secular, the intensest self-consciousness, the feeling of personality, predominates. Poetry is no longer objective, epic, and naïf; it is subjective, lyrical, and reflective."

---

[7] *Page* 81.

John Tauler was born at Strasburg in 1290. In 1308 he entered the Dominican order, and for some time studied theology at Paris. On his return to his native city he came under the influence of Master Eckhart, called "the Father of German Speculation," and the most celebrated of the so-called mystics of the Middle Ages. Whilst, however, the mysticism of Eckhart led to quietism, Tauler's whole life was spent in practical religious activity. He was the greatest preacher of his time, and is even held by some writers to have been the greatest preacher of Mediæval times. When about fifty years of age, Tauler was brought under an influence more powerful than that of Eckhart, namely, that of Nicolas of Basle, who was styled "the Friend of God." At the instigation of Nicolas, Tauler passed two years in religious seclusion and in the practice of the severest ascetic discipline. He then resumed his preaching, braved the interdict laid by Pope John XXII. on Strasburg, and the horrors of the "black death" that devastated the city in 1348. Obliged for a time to betake himself to Cologne, he afterwards returned to Strasburg, and died there in 1361. Besides the three volumes of sermons published at Frankfort in 1826, many of Tauler's homilies still remain unprinted. The authenticity of the sacred songs attributed to him is doubtful.

[8] *Page* 83.

William Law, author of the " Serious Call to a Devout and Holy Life," was the English translator and expositor of Jacob Böhme's works. Jane Lead, one of the most celebrated of English mystics, possessed an intimate acquaintance with Böhme's writings,—an acquaintance obtained probably through Dr. John Pordage, who presided over an English society of " Illuminati." In 1697 Jane Lead founded the sect of the " Philadelphians," of which Francis Lee, the poet of mysticism, was a member. Such was the influence of Böhme's works and system of theosophy in this country. But far more remarkable is the influence they exercised on German philosophy. Schelling, though reluctant to admit the fact, owed much to the writings of the shoemaker of Görlitz. Hegel not only acknowledged that the title " Philosophicus Teutonicus " had been justly bestowed on Böhme, from whom he dates the beginning of modern philosophy, but he also declares his substantial agreement with Böhme's first principles. Louis Claude de Saint Martin (1743–1803), called " Le Philosophe Inconnue," translated into French Böhme's first work " Aurora." Franz Xaver von Baader (1765–1841) was the most recent German expositor of Böhme, though his own speculations were of far too original a nature to permit of his being styled a disciple of Böhme.

---

[9] *Page* 124.

Mr. Adamson's rendering of the term *Wissenschaftslehre* is here gratefully adopted, though, as he justly says, we have no English equivalent for the German. In the French version of " Religion and Philosophy in Germany," *Wissenschaftslehre* is very inadequately translated *Doctrine de la*

Science. In his excellent short biography of Fichte (Black-wood's Philosophical Classics), Mr. Adamson does not fail to do justice to what Heine calls the social significance of Fichte. In his introductory chapter he says : " There exists not now, there never did exist to any extent, a school of followers of Fichte; it may well be doubted if there are at present half-a-dozen students of his works. As a patriot, as a representative of what seems noblest and loftiest in the German character, he lives, and will doubtless continue to live, in the grateful remembrance of his countrymen ; as a metaphysician, he lives not at all beyond the pages of the historians of philosophy."

---

[10] *Page* 142.

J. H. Rosenmüller (1736–1815), a celebrated German preacher. In 1785 he was appointed pastor of the Thomaskirche, and a professor of theology at the University of Leipzig. His most important service to his age and country consisted in the improvements he was the means of bringing about in the methods of teaching in the schools at Leipzig. His voluminous writings are partly of a devotional and partly of a critical character. Heine was here probably referring either to the " Scholia in Novum Testamentum " or to the " Historia interpretationis Librorum Sacrorum in Ecclesia Christiana."

---

[11] *Page* 144.

Peter Andreas Heiberg, dramatist and political writer, was born at Bordinborg, in Denmark, in 1758. Banished from his native country on account of his political opinions, he betook himself to Paris, where a great part of his life was spent. During the First Empire he held an appointment in the French Foreign Office, and at the Restoration he was awarded a pension. He died at Paris in 1841. Heiberg's fame rests chiefly on his comedies, of which 'Heckingborn' is the best known. He also wrote 'Political Aphorisms,' and a 'Précis Historique et Critique de la Constitution de la Monarchie Danoise' (Paris, 1820). In imitation of the Letters of Junius, he wrote 'Lettres d'un Norvégien de la Vielle Roche' (Paris, 1822).

---

[12] *Page* 144.

John George Forster was born near Danzig in 1754. At an early age he accompanied his father, John Reinhold Forster, the traveller and naturalist, to Russia. Father and son afterwards came to England, where the former settled for a time as a teacher of languages at Warrington. In 1772 John Reinhold Forster was appointed naturalist to Captain Cook's second expedition, and was again accompanied by his son, who in 1777 published an account of the expedition ("A Voyage Round the World in His Britannic Majesty's Sloop *Resolution*"). After holding during several years a professorship of natural history, first at Cassel and afterwards at Wilna in Germany, John George Forster was called to Mainz, as librarian to the Elector, in 1788. On the taking of Mainz by the French in 1792, Forster, who had become deeply imbued with the principles of the Revolution, was sent to Paris as the deputy of his like-minded fellow-townsmen to sue for the union of their city with the French Republic. He died at Paris in 1794. Forster's political career is treated as material by H. Hoenig in his novel "Die Clubisten in Mainz."

---

[13] *Page* 158.

At this point the first German edition comes to a close. What follows was struck out by the censor. It is restored in the later editions. A portion of Heine's remarkable prophecy has already been fulfilled in the events of 1870–1871. The fantastic and reactionary policy of Prince Bismarck seems not unlikely to aid in bringing about that catastrophe in Germany "compared to which the French revolution will seem but an innocent idyl." It is to this singular prophecy, in part already fulfilled and in part perhaps about to be fulfilled, that Heine refers in the "Preface to the Second German Edition." (See page 10 of the present volume.)